Essays on Martin Luther's Theology of Music

Essays on
Martin Luther's
Theology of Music

Mark S. Sooy

Published by Blue Maroon

Essays on Martin Luther's Theology of Music
Mark S. Sooy

Published by Blue Maroon
in cooperation with Booklocker.com, Inc.

For more information about this book, the author, or other available resources visit www.blue-maroon.com.

For U.B. and A.M.
whose generosity allowed me
the opportunity to study and grow.

Contents

Acknowledgments

Many thanks to the men and women who have taught me the importance of the theological task and to love God's Word. Especially to Dr. Ed Wishart, Dr. Dale DeWitt, Dr. Michael Wittmer, and Dr. Byard Bennett who were unrelenting in their pursuit of God's truth and pushed me to seek that truth with passion and perseverance.

For the men, women and children of New Song Ministries who allowed me to teach and preach about the significance of Luther's theology and thought. Even if you never read this volume, you have heard much of what is here. Thank you for the opportunity to grow with you in grace and the knowledge of God.

To Gene Pearson, who helped to proofread this manuscript. Thank you for your friendship and thoroughness. You are truly appreciated.

To D. Martin Luther. He will never know how much his writings influenced my theology and Christian walk until I am able to tell him myself, as we stand in the presence of Christ. Luther always pointed me toward Christ – it will be a pleasure to finally meet him rejoicing before the throne of our Savior and worship Him side-by-side.

Thanks to my parents, Gordon & Irene Sooy, and my two brothers and their wives: Brian & Lisa Sooy and Eric & Julie Sooy. Thanks for watching, praying and helping us along the way in this life of ministry.

And thanks to my wife, Elisabeth, and our children: Estelle, Ashlea, and Gordon. Their support and encouragement throughout the research and writing process was gracious and enthusiastic. Thank you for being patient. You are the best.

Introduction

A major influence

Martin Luther's theology has had a profound effect on my own theology. The clarity I have found in reading his works has literally transformed my theological outlook. The greatest area of his influence has been on how theology intersects with our daily lives, and how every part of our theology is built upon other parts.

I have no intention of declaring Luther's thinking as the "perfect" theology. He was a man – in search of God and seeking to serve Him with all that he was – but a man like the rest of us. There is plenty in his theology and thought that I not yet fully considered, and given there are fifty-three volumes of his writings in English, I have only really scratched the surface in understanding what he wrote.

What I have found is that his presentation of theology is one of the most balanced I have ever read. He was relentless in conforming his own beliefs and theology to Scripture, and then taking those to the people and the church. The constant development of his theology is staggering as he studied, learned, and grew in his own faith. I suppose this is what I mean by "balance" – the willingness and ability to allow Scripture to form and transform your beliefs and your life on a continuing basis. It is a balance of perspective – God's perspective.

Because of my interest and experience in music and worship, it was fitting for me to do an in-depth study of Luther's views on these subjects and bring these two worlds together. I expected to find some poignant information similar to what I have found in modern discussions, but I actually found something unexpected.

Rather than starting with "music" or with "worship" as so many studies do, Luther's views were shaped by a much broader (and balanced) view of creation and the work of God in His creation. This adds a depth to his thoughts that is seldom approached today. He does not consider worship or music (or anything else) except upon a foundation of a deep and rich understanding of God and His revelation of Himself – in the Bible and in Jesus Christ. Luther allows the fabric of his theology to be thick with interconnected strings and threads. To consider his views on one matter, we must consider his views on many other matters as well.

Direction

The other major area of influence that Martin Luther has had on me was to point me to Scripture. As much as I enjoy his writings, I have always realized that they point me back to the Bible – and more specifically in his own language – they point me to Christ. I have read many, many books, articles, and commentaries and listened to a lot of music over the years. Nothing has motivated me more to look to Christ and Scripture than Luther's writings.

And so, I find myself driven to understand. I am not satisfied with the overabundance of shallow explanations of worship and music found in the church today. There is more to it than finding some texts to prove the validity for using contemporary music, or allowing the pragmatic considerations of modern society to dictate what worship is and how it is to be practiced. It is deeper and broader than this, and is wrapped with theological overtones and undertones that are seldom considered.

I am driven to know and understand those theological overtones and undertones. I want to delve into Scripture and see what it is saying – not just the verses about worship specifically – but also those verses that are not about worship, per se, but in fact have much to do with worship.

Background Matters

The type of analysis and presentation found in the following pages is done with a significant amount of background research and study. Research and study develop our thoughts and theology in an ongoing effort to know God and Scripture better. As a result, there are certain assumptions made and conclusions drawn by the author which find their way into a book, yet are only explained in summary form. I know this to be the case in what I have written.

In my own experience, I sometimes wonder how an author or commentator has come to the convictions and beliefs he or she has written about. Occasionally, an author will give sufficient background material to satisfy my curiosity. More often than not I find myself in search of another book or article by the same author that will shed light on what I had already read.

After re-reading the manuscript for my book, *The Life of Worship: Rethink, Reform, Renew*, I thought it would be appropriate to include some type of background material to help the interested reader see part of the journey I took to come to the set of convictions concerning personal and corporate worship found in that volume. Of course, the journey began over twenty years ago and continues even today, so what I include here is only a part of the process. This current volume, *Essays on Martin Luther's Theology of Music*, is intended to give you a glimpse into the formation of my "theology of worship" found in the pages of *The Life of Worship*.

This particular set of studies is somewhat more academic and technical than the presentation in *The Life of Worship*. I have separated these essays from the other book for two reasons: *The Life of Worship* can and does stand alone as a full consideration of my thoughts on worship. For those satisfied with what was written in that work, the following pages may not be necessary. Second, because *Essays* is more academic, it will take a good deal more commitment to read and understand what is being considered. I believe it to be an important study, and one that will help reinforce what I have already written. For those, like me, who always like more information – read on!

Chapter 1 is a basic overview of how the Reformers viewed music and an example of Luther's imbedding of theological concepts into a hymn. Chapters 2 through 4 are in depth and detailed discussions of Luther's theology of music itself, and some comparative considerations with Calvin. Chapter 5 draws everything together and seeks to provide a demonstration of Luther's balanced view of theology and music, as well as a challenge to the current state of theology regarding music. Finally, Chapter 6 is somewhat of a "bonus" chapter about Luther's doctrine of the Word of God. This concept is mentioned throughout the previous chapters and will help to give a broader perspective.

Writing my book titled *The Life of Worship* was my way to participate and engage in the process of theological development. This volume of *Essays on Martin Luther's Theology of Music* is some of the background that drives me in this continuing process. I would encourage you to read it carefully and understand the implications of what it might mean for your own study and theology on worship and music for the church.

Chapter 1

Discovering the Theology of the Reformers in Their Hymns

A study of Protestant hymnody and hymn usage is an enormous undertaking. There are many factors that have influenced the music of Protestant churches dating back to its earliest beginnings during the Reformation. Each of the magisterial Reformers had their unique thoughts on the use of music within the liturgy (i.e., the church service) and this affected the hymn styles and song collections of the various Protestant groups. As the Reformation progressed and matured the unique characteristics of each viewpoint became clearer.

The focus of this essay is to discover how the theology of the Reformers is reflected in their hymns. Although interest concerning worship in general has increased in recent years, the connection of *theology* with *hymnody* is an area of study that continues to need attention. As Teresa Berger pointed out, "in spite of the importance of hymn traditions for the life of practically all Christian communities (both liturgical and non-liturgical), theological reflection on hymns remains a stepchild of scholarly inquiry."[1] Nevertheless, hymn writing and hymn singing was an important aspect of the Reformation and one which helps us understand that era of Church History. In addition, we will examine how various Reformers viewed music in general, since this directly influenced their hymnody (i.e., what they allowed to be used as congregational song).

Let us first consider how the overall belief systems and theological convictions of three of the major Reformers influenced the use of hymns within the church and as part of the liturgy. We will look at the views of those who have had the greatest impact upon Protestant Christianity in this area: Martin Luther, John Calvin and Huldrych Zwingli.

Martin Luther

Martin Luther had the broadest views of music of any of the Reformers. James White notes that Luther's "liturgical reform was guided by the principle that if the Scriptures did not expressly reject a particular practice, the church was free to keep it."[2] Luther thought music to be a gift from God and considered it of the highest importance next to the preaching of the Word (i.e., theology). He saw congregational singing as a vital part of church life, and made the singing of hymns in the language of the common people a hallmark of the German Reformation. He also encouraged others to do the same, enlisting help in building a hymnody for the common people. In writing to his friend Spalatin in 1524, Luther encouraged his input for hymns in the German language, "[Our] plan is to follow the example of the prophets and the ancient fathers of the church, and to compose psalms for the people [in the] vernacular, that is, spiritual songs, so that the Word of God may be among the people also in the form of music."[3]

Luther was concerned for the common people under his care. He wanted them to have God's Word in language they could understand. The reason for this was that most of the general population during this period of history could not read or write. Music and lyrics were an excellent way to help them remember important Christian truths. In another letter, asking for a translation of a psalm, Luther wrote, "I would ask you, however, to avoid new words and the expression of the courts, so that the people may easily understand. Let the words be as simple as possible but at the same time pure and suitable; and see that the meaning be clear and as close to that of the psalms. We must therefore use our own judgment, determine the original meaning, and translate it freely."[4]

Luther thought highly enough of the importance of hymns that he wrote numerous hymns himself – being a quite gifted singer and lute player. He also rewrote both ancient and common hymns of the day, as well as writing sacred texts for tunes used in everyday life.[5]

For Luther, church music had a three-fold purpose:
1) the praise of God;
2) an offering of the congregation; and
3) Christian education of humanity.[6]

This is a very broad understanding of the use of music in the church, and obviously comes from his time spent in the study of the Psalms, which also show these purposes in the use of music in the congregation of Israel.

In general, Luther allowed music of all kinds to be an integral part of church life. For him it was another tool to be used in the teaching of the Word of God. His personal love of music, his love of his Savior, and his love of the people were all naturally expressed through song. As Paul Nettle observes, "The jubilant faith of Luther, his joyful experience of God, his teaching of salvation by grace, caused him to break out in exultation before his God, and his feeling could find expression only in music."[7]

John Calvin

John Calvin had a somewhat narrower view of music and especially of the hymnody to be used by the congregation. Although he appreciated and encouraged the use of all forms of music *outside* the church and the liturgy, both vocal and instrumental, *within* the liturgy he allowed only the use of unaccompanied unison Psalms.[8] Under his guidance and influence the Swiss Reformation produced the *Genevan Psalter*, which eventually included metrical versions of all 150 Psalms as well as other biblical texts. This "metrical psalmody" was (and continues to be) the defining mark of the liturgy of the Reformed Church.

The stark simplicity of Calvinist Worship was not negative at all, but was an attempt to solve one of the fundamental questions concerning freedom raised by the Reformation, namely, the relation of freedom to the world. Under the new sense of the significance of freedom a new import was given to the truth that the only acceptable worship is that of the heart, and that the intrusion of the merely material attraction is a degradation of its pure service. The best worship penetrates to that region where the things of sense cannot accompany men; where, with nothing to speak to the senses, the Eternal God in purest spirit is present in His supersensible glory.[9]

Thus, unaccompanied unison singing was the purest form of music and eliminated any possibility of distraction from instruments or other vocal parts. This allowed the people to concentrate on the spiritual meaning of the words, and not get caught up in the technicalities of the music.

For Calvin, worship was God's activity among the people in the liturgy. John Witvliet explains that "this divine action was construed in Trinitarian terms, where Christ is 'the chief conductor of our hymns (i.e., psalms),' the one who 'hallows our lips...to sing the praises of God,' while the Holy Spirit is the prompter who urges the people to sing."[10] This helps us understand why Calvin limited music in the church to that of the Psalms. The Psalms were considered the purest form of lyric coming directly from the hand of God. Hymns (such as used by the Lutherans) were prohibited. E. E. Ryden observes that this prohibition was put in place because these hymns were "the production of men. God could be worshipped in a worthy manner, according to Calvin's principles, only by hymns which were divinely inspired, namely the psalms of the Old Testament Psalter."[11]

Like Luther, Calvin saw the use of music within the liturgy as a means of praising God, but unlike Luther, not as a tool in teaching the congregation. Again, Witvliet notes, "The Psalms were not sung primarily for didactic purposes but rather, for the congregation to extol God."[12] In limiting its use, Calvin molded the Reformed style, and function, of music within the liturgy. And this continues to be the dominant view in some Reformed circles today.

Huldrych Zwingli

Even narrower than the perspective of John Calvin were the views of Huldrych Zwingli – the Reformer based in Zurich. Zwingli basically omitted music as a whole from the liturgy. In his study titled *Zwingli and the Arts*, Charles Garside gives an excellent synopsis of Zwingli's thought concerning music. In Zwingli's view, liturgical music was "scripturally indefensible on three closely interrelated, yet distinguishable, grounds:

> 1)   Music in worship is not explicitly commanded by God in either the Old or New Testament.
> 2)   Christ instructed men to pray to God individually and in private. (John 4:24)
> 3)   Saint Paul urged men, when together, to worship God and pray to Him in their hearts. (Colossians 3:16)"[13]

Zwingli's focus on prayer, as the purest form of worship, dominated his view of liturgical forms. The liturgy was simple and straightforward. Donald Hustad explains, "Zwinglian liturgy tended to be more didactic than devotional. His typical morning service resembled the ancient Prone liturgy, consisting of Scripture reading (Epistle and Gospel), preaching, and a long prayer."[14] This was seen as a pure Pauline form of worship. Music simply had no place.

This attitude toward music in worship led to a sharp distinction between what Zwingli thought to be "true worship" (private, individual prayer), and the "hypocritical liturgy" (public, external show) of the Catholic Church. Garside notes, "The choral and instrumental music of the contemporary Catholic Church was full of the repetition of many words. Furthermore, it had become increasingly a matter of display before men, frequently a dazzling display of the technical abilities not only of the performer, but of the composer."[15] Zwingli sought for pure worship in focusing and communicating with God in prayer. He writes, "But when we wish to pray we should withdraw into our chamber and close the door after us and there, in secret, call upon our heavenly Father."[16] Charles Garside comments on this statement:

> With that sentence Zwingli reveals the extremity of his reach. What he seeks is nothing less than an irreducible purity of worship—in other words, an absolutely private prayer: the individual withdrawn from the world and from his fellow men, absolutely alone in communion with his heavenly Father. The Father's Son has commanded such worship. Therefore, ideally, no other form should be considered, for no other form would accord so literally with the law of Christ. Thus Christ's instructions stand at the very core of Zwingli's liturgical thinking, from out of which all else radiates and without which the external forms in which his liturgy was finally cast cannot be comprehended...
>
> Such an ideal could scarcely be realized, however, if the communal worship of the visible Church is to be observed and retained, and this for Zwingli was a necessity beyond dispute. The content of prayer must be given some formal, ritual expression in public. Yet once worship is made public, full opportunity is immediately provided for countless varieties of hypocrisy and display.[17]

Interestingly enough, Zwingli himself was a very accomplished musician and could play virtually any instrument he desired. His personal theology simply would not allow the use of music in church, and to that conviction he was true. This conviction was so important that he even had the organs in the cathedrals of Zurich removed!

Having finished this short and elemental discussion of the theological views of music and its liturgical use in these three Reformers we find a quite diverse representation. For Luther, all music was appropriate—Psalms, hymns, instrumental music. For Calvin, only some, and only that which was biblically based—metrical Psalms. And for Zwingli, no music was appropriate for truly pure worship.

Analysis of "A Mighty Fortress is our God"

With this diversity in mind, we turn to consider the actual theological convictions of the Reformers as discovered in their hymns (at least those who used hymns!). The best place to turn for this part of the study is Martin Luther, since there is such a rich field of texts and songs to study. Considered the father of Protestant hymnody, the examination of one of his hymns will give us the best perspective on how hymns were used to pass on important aspects of theology, at least in the German Reformation. Remember, Calvin only allowed the used of Psalms and Scripture texts which dictated what theological elements would appear in the congregational songs. Though certainly not exhaustive, this will give us a good indication and example how Luther passed Christian truth to the common people and his followers.

Berenard Kreuzer observed, "Hymnody is 'theology.' As a form of art, synthesizing both literature and music, it is not necessarily always in accord with dogmatic theology, however. When the hymnody does not mirror faithfully the dogmatic theology of a Church, then we find that it mirrors the practical theology of the people."[18] This is true of Martin Luther's hymn *A Mighty Fortress is our God.* We will be analyzing the translation by Frederick H. Hedge, which is the most popular in the United States. The text is as follows:

A mighty fortress is our God, A bulwark never failing;
Our helper He amid the flood Of mortal ills prevailing.
For still our ancient foe Doth seek to work us woe—
His craft and power are great, And, armed with cruel hate,
On earth is not his equal.

Did we in our own strength confide,
Our striving would be losing,
Were not the right man on our side,
The man of God's own choosing.
Dost ask who that may be? Christ Jesus, it is He—
Lord Sabaoth His name, From age to age the same,

11

And He must win the battle.

And though this world, with devils filled,
Should threaten to undo us,
We will not fear, for God hath willed
His truth to triumph through us.
The prince of darkness grim, We tremble not for him—
His rage we can endure, For lo, his doom is sure:
One little word shall fell him.

That word above all earthly powers,
No thanks to them, abideth;
the Spirit and the gifts are ours
Through Him who with us sideth.
Let goods and kindred go, This mortal life also—
The body they may kill; God's truth abideth still:
His kingdom is forever.

We must note that Luther used Psalm 46 as the basis for this hymn. It could almost be considered a "jump-off point" from which he then constructed the flow of the verses – moving from one to the other to complete the thought of the whole song. It touches on aspects of theology and life that would instruct, admonish and encourage both those who sang and those who heard the message. Though referencing another of Luther's hymns (*Lord, Keep Us Steadfast in Your Word*), the following quote from Oliver Rupprecht can equally be applied here:

Unless we sense these psychological and emotional elements—founded on Scripture and emphasized by the vivid and suggestive power of music—we are missing many of the riches of this song. Rightly considered, they are riches of a theological kind. Properly used, the psychological and emotional elements stimulated and supplied by musical tones can serve as valuable adjuncts to the verbal message: they can help equip the mind and empower the soul for victory in the struggle of divinely-given powers against forces that cause disaster and disarray.[19]

In our analysis we will simply point to the major theological concepts represented in *A Mighty Fortress is Our God.*

First, we can find references to the power and majesty of God. This is evident in His person (a *mighty fortress,* a *bulwark*), as well as His intervention and providence in our lives (our *helper amid mortal ills,* the *right man on our side, He must win the battle* – not us). His power can also be seen in His triumph over Satan (*God has willed His truth to triumph through us*) and over death (*let goods and kindred go, this mortal life also, etc. – His kingdom is forever.*)

Second, notice the Christological focus of the hymn. Christ is *the right man on our side* (note the reference to His humanity), chosen by God. He is also the *Lord Sabaoth* (note the reference to His divinity), everlasting (*age to age the same*), and the ultimate warrior against Satan (and *He must win the battle*), winning the battle on our behalf.

Third, we can note the reminder of the inability of man to provide for his own salvation. We need help (*our helper amid the flood*). We are weaker than our foe and enemy (*on earth is not his equal*). We cannot count on our own strength to deliver us (*Did we in our own strength confide, Our striving would be losing*). We have no need to fear, for God will triumph through us. And again, Christ is on our side (*through Him who with us sideth*) to conquer sin, death and the Devil.

Fourth is the recognition of the reality of Satan and his forces. He is *our ancient foe,* seeking to harm us (*Doth seek to work us woe*) and *armed with cruel hate.* He is powerful and mighty beyond human abilities (*his craft and power are great,* and *on earth is not his equal*). The world is filled with his forces (*though the world with devils filled*), and they seek to harm us as well (*should threaten to undo us*).

Fifth, we find references to each person of the Trinity. God is the *mighty fortress.* Christ Jesus is the warrior conqueror in our battle with Satan. And the Holy Spirit is the One who endows us with gifts, as a result of Christ's work on our behalf

(*The Spirit and the gifts are ours through Him who with us sideth*).

Overall, we can find – even in this short analysis – that Martin Luther filled this hymn with profound theological concepts and references. No doubt that in a full study of Luther's hymns we would find a complete representation of many more ideas which Luther sought to pass on to the people through the use of congregational song. Other groups that used hymns (the Anabaptists for example) in their liturgies also used hymns in similar ways, as well as passing on in song traditions specific to the group.

In conclusion, we have found a very diverse representation of the use of hymns and music within the Reformation. Though this study has been limited, it has given us a good indication of how the Reformers viewed music as used in the church as well as how some passed on their theology in congregational song.

Chapter 2

Luther's Theology of Music

Martin Luther's significance in the reshaping of Christian theology and molding a theology based upon the five *sola* statements (*sola scriptura, sola fide, sola gratia, sola cristo, sola Deo gloria*) is widely recognized. His theology is broad, and the various ways in which he rethinks and modifies areas of theology – doctrine, church authority and structure, social concerns and others – touch every part of life and are quite expansive. Research into Luther's thought is as deep as it is wide, and yet there is evidence that in the midst of all of this research, Luther's thought is wider and deeper still.

One area that scholars have missed, or only hinted at, is how Luther's theology in the arena of creation has informed and molded his theology of the arts. Many have recognized in Luther's thought the connection between God as the Creator and man who is creative as a result of being made in God's image – especially as he is re-made (redeemed) in Christ.[20] However, only Brian L. Horne has observed that Luther's thought on music is built upon his reading of the creation account in Genesis, and his comments are limited to one paragraph in a larger discussion.[21] The next few chapters will pursue this idea in greater depth by considering Luther's statements on the use and function of the arts (especially music) side by side with the essentials of his doctrine of creation. In so doing we will seek to draw further conclusions concerning Luther's commitment to, and inclusion of, the arts for the church.

Music and Creation in Luther's Thought

Though lengthy, it is helpful to begin with Horne's answer to the question, "What does Luther believe to be the truth about the importance of music?" Horne responds in this way:

> There are many clues scattered throughout his work, but the most interesting is, perhaps, found in the exegesis he provided of the opening chapters of Genesis. In discussing the nature of God's creative activity, Luther's mind revolved around the question of order. These opening chapters of the Bible tell the story of the establishment of order in the original creation of the world, and the destruction of that order by the rebellion of Adam. The creation of the world is, for Luther, the revelation of a divine order in the life and purpose of God himself. The Word, through which the world is made, and the world itself, do not appear as two different kinds of revelation; they are part of a single revelation of the divine order which is in the mind of the Creator. In the aftermath of the terrible disruption of that order by the sin of Adam two things remain: theology and music. Why music? For Luther the entirely non-figurative, non-representational, non-verbal world of sound in which every note and rhythm finds its proper place in the whole, and is indispensable to the whole, was not only a sign of the possibility of order, but was an actual achievement of that order, a sure indication of the stability of God in a shifting and unstable world. It seems clear from everything he said that he could not have borne a world without music: 'I hope my life is nearly at an end (this was in 1530), for the world hates me and I am sick of it...So I keep humming this canticle.' Music in its utterly formal arrangement of sound was a means of holding the chaos of life at bay, of imposing order upon the frighteningly disparate pieces of experience. In a world without music chaos is come again.[22]

Besides Horne, other authors only mention this subject in passing when they refer to God's creative nature and music as a gift of the creative God, never really delving into the foundations of it as found in Luther's concept of creation. Paul Althaus generalizes this idea in the following observation:

> God 'showers us with his own being.' He gives us what he is. For Luther, God's sharing of himself is the highest expression of the fact that God is God. It means that the attributes of God are by their very nature creative and are not only his own and remain in himself but are also shared with men. Luther feels that this is true of all God's attributes. Luther first became aware of this in the biblical concept of the righteousness of God...All of God's attributes therefore describe an activity in which God shares himself with men and allows them to participate in his being. God brings this about in Christ.[23]

God's creativity, therefore, is passed on to man as seen in his creative endeavors in the artistic world. To suppress that creativity in man is to suppress the very image of God found in man and redeemed in Christ. Even in this short synopsis, one can see a connection in Luther's thought between the arts and creation.

It is commonly acknowledged by scholars that Luther's theology of the arts, and of music in particular, is quite accepting and open-ended. His attitude was that if Scripture did not forbid it, then it was acceptable (and redeemable) for use by the church in its worship of God. Charles Garside notes, "Luther...placed few, if any, such limitation either on text or music. So long as musicians and poets, separately or together, were enriching the liturgy to a 'pious use,' their imaginative faculties were unrestricted."[24] It was this open and accepting valuation of the arts that led to the rich and diverse heritage of German protestant music, for example, in such composers at Bach, Haydn, Handel and others. Luther's impact upon German culture in this manner is truly remarkable and shows his influence was much broader in the society than purely as a theologian and reformer. This is in stark contrast to the arrested development of the arts within other parts of the

Reformed tradition, especially within the influence of Calvin, but even more so in that of Zwingli.[25]

The Focus and Importance of This Study

It seems then, that Luther's theology concerning the arts, especially music, is intertwined with his doctrine of creation. One cannot truly understand his openness for the artistic endeavor (in all of its forms) unless at a more basic level a foundation is laid for his holistic approach to, and understanding of, creation. God created the whole man, the whole man is infected by sin, and the whole man is redeemed in Christ. Music swirls around this holistic ideal in Luther's mind, as well as how music itself reflects creation, fall and redemption and the re-establishment of the created order. There seems to be more to this than current scholarship has thus far revealed and a study of these areas of Luther's thought, side by side, will be quite beneficial.

This study will first consider the foundational characteristics of Luther's theology concerning creation, especially as he finds in it the evidence of *order*. From that foundation, parallels and connections will be drawn between Luther's creation theology and his theology of music.[26]

Secondly, a discussion and comparison of Luther's views of music with both Calvin's and Zwingli's will help to put his theology into the broader context of the Reformation and the thought of the major Reformers.

Finally, a short synopsis of the major points will be presented followed by a discussion considering why this study is important and pertinent to the church today, especially in its ongoing development and use of creativity in music and worship.

Chapter 3

Creation and Music

As a man of his time, Martin Luther was trained and educated in late medieval thought (i.e., late scholasticism and nominalism), beginning in his earliest days as a schoolboy and continuing into his university studies in Erfurt and Wittenburg. There is debate among scholars whether his mind was entrenched in that mode of thought or whether he broke free of it in many significant ways. It is quite characteristic of Luther to glean the best of what a system of thought had to offer, based upon its subordination to the Word of God, and transform it for his own theological framework. Regardless, there is a foundation that was laid in his training and education that must be considered in order to understand how histheology of creation is related to his theology of music.

This chapter will discuss the medieval scholastic background in which Luther was educated and his ties to nominalistic thinking, including observations about his use and adaptation of nominalist principles. Augustine's influence on Luther (he was, after all, an Augustinian monk) will also be considered, as he was a significant force in the development of the entirety of Luther's theology. This will be followed by an analysis of Luther's theology of creation as found throughout his commentary on Genesis chapters one through three, especially as he discovers the evidence of an ordered creation. Finally, some salient points will be developed on how interrelated his views on creation are with his views of music.

Luther and Medieval Thought: Faith and Reason

One significant aspect of medieval theology was its focus on the appropriate understanding between *faith* and *reason*.[27] This background is important as it recognizes the impact of medieval thought on Luther. For example, one major theme in Luther's theology is the distinction between law and gospel. Law, or the general pursuit of righteousness by human endeavor, is that which condemns the sinner, for "*by the works of the law shall no flesh be justified*" before God (Romans 3:20). The medieval church was trapped in this mode of thinking in which man sought to justify himself and his actions before God and, according to Luther, *reason* played an important part in this. *Reason* and *law* walked hand in hand as humans attempted to gain God's favor – and thus earn their own salvation.

The gospel, however, was Luther's word for describing how the righteousness of God comes to the sinner, by God's grace as a gift, through *faith* in Jesus Christ (Romans 3:22). Christ takes the sinner's sin and gives the sinner His own righteousness, in what is referred to as the "joyous exchange." *Faith* is the key in understanding the gospel, and in some ways this joyous exchange makes no sense to reason, which for Luther makes reason suspect in its ability to understand the ways of God. This connection between *gospel* and *faith* is noteworthy and significant in Luther's thought and draws them together in unity of purpose.

Even in this short summary of one major underlying presupposition of Luther's theology, that of the distinction between *law and gospel*, one can see the connection and parallel with *faith* and *reason*. Man's sin has corrupted the created order. In his *reason*, man seeks to restore that order, but is unable to do so for only in Christ, by *faith*, can that order truly be restored (redeemed). These concepts will be more clearly drawn together in the coming pages, but suffice it to say that, in Luther's mind, there is a direct link between music, as evidence of order, and redemption of that order in Christ by faith. It is therefore pertinent that one understands Luther's background and thought in the *faith/reason* debate.

The neo-Platonic, Augustinian view that "Faith seeks Understanding" was considered to be the appropriate relationship of *faith* and *reason* early in the medieval period and during the rise of scholastic thought. Referred to as Realism, faith was necessary and superior to reason, and reason served faith in its quest for God. Examples of this are found in such scholars as Anselm of Canterbury and societies such as the Franciscans. Etienne Gilson observes that the implications from "Augustine's explicit statement [are], first that we are invited by Revelation itself to believe, that unless we believe we shall not understand; next that far from inviting us to do away with reason, the Gospel itself has promised to all those who seek truth in the revealed word the reward of understanding."[28] *Faith* and *reason* (revelation and philosophy) are united in this form of scholasticism, with faith quite distinctively holding the upper hand.

As the medieval period progressed, the climax of scholastic thought was found in the writings of Thomas Aquinas and the society of the Dominicans. Structurally based on Aristotelian philosophy, the *faith/reason* relationship was thought to be best balanced in the recognition that faith was necessary for understanding those things which are supernatural by nature, but reason could stand by itself in the discovery and knowledge of all things natural (i.e., natural theology). Called Moderate Realism, faith was necessary for the highest articles of theology, whereas reason (alone) could discover the lower articles. *Faith* and *reason* (revelation and philosophy) are compatible, but in some senses quite separate, in this form of scholasticism. It is a scheme of thought seeking a balance between the two, but also, as Gilson notes, trying to "take philosophy for what it is: the knowledge of what man would hold as true, if absolute truth had not been given to him by the divine Revelation."[29]

Also of major concern within this middle period of medieval scholasticism (and holding on even through the Reformation) was the matter of *order*. In general terms, the scholastics (especially as articulated by Aquinas) sought as their ideal the *rightly ordered* man. This is one in whom the natural faculties and virtues (i.e., intellect, will, external and internal senses, and natural appetites) are *ordered*, or controlled, properly due to the influence of the theological virtues given by grace in redemption. This influence of the theological virtues is referred to as the *donum super additum*, or extra added gift of grace. Once this gift is received, reason is restored and able to practice natural theology, as well as control (*order*) the natural faculties and virtues, without any further assistance from faith. Faith essentially serves as the vehicle through which reason is restored (redeemed) to its original condition, and thus able to function as God intended. In this philosophical structure, reason is raised to a level of importance at least equal to faith, and, some would say, over and above faith.

Toward the end of the medieval period, during late scholasticism's decline, *reason* was found to be untrustworthy altogether. All that was necessary to know, both naturally and supernaturally, was to be discovered by *faith*. *Faith* and *reason* (revelation and philosophy) were separate and reason was rejected in regards to all things theological (in other words, natural theology was not possible). Duns Scotus, and especially William of Ockham, are representative of this period of scholasticism which became known as the "via moderna" – the modern way (ultimately called Nominalism as it finds its expression especially in Ockham). This method denied "the possibility of a rational demonstration of the truths of 'natural' religion," and regarded "revelation as something arbitrary, to be accepted with unreasoning submissions and left without comment or explanation."[30] It was an extreme reaction on the progressive side of scholastic thought, balancing the other extreme reaction to scholasticism: Christian humanism as represented in the writings of Erasmus. As a model for Christian thought, scholasticism unraveled in the light of these new systems, and Luther found fertile ground for his mind to work.

Another aspect of influence on Luther's thought is his exposure to and understanding of Augustine's writings. That *order* is so significant in his treatment of the creation account reflects Augustine's comments in *The Nature of the Good* when he writes, "These three things, *measure, form* and *order*, not to mention innumerable other things which demonstrably belong to them, are as it were generic good things to be found in all that God has created, whether spirit or body."[31] Luther picks up on the idea that order is one of the "good things" of creation (as declared by God) and there is also evidence that he adhered to the fullness of Augustine's concept of measure, form and order – as will be noted later. Order, then, for Luther, demonstrates the goodness in which God created, as well as the goodness of creation itself.

It was in the atmosphere of late medieval scholasticism and nominalism that Luther received his education. He even called William of Ockham his "master" at one point, though this was only through the influence of his writings. This educational inheritance, including the influence of Augustine, was to be foundational to Luther's development of Reformation principles. Among other things, it led him to return to Scripture as the final authority of revelation, as it did John Wyclif and his followers.[32] From this basis Luther forms his thoughts concerning creation – how it is ordered and flows from the care and providence of God.

Primary Data:
Luther's Commentary on Genesis 1-3

Luther expresses the principles concerning order in his commentary on Genesis chapters one through three. First, we find a glimpse into the nominalism that affects his thought as he writes about the "days" and "evenings" of creation being "without allegory." According to Luther's interpretation, and his dependence upon Scripture as the authoritative revelation, one is to consider Moses' purpose to "teach us, not about allegorical creatures and an allegorical world but about real creatures and a visible world apprehended by the senses. Therefore, as the proverb has it, he calls 'a spade a spade,' i.e., he employs the terms 'day' and 'evening' without allegory, just as we customarily do."[33] The nominalistic influence here is indicated in Luther's comment about the "world apprehended by the senses." The nominalist view of reality was in the particulars – in the actual things of creation. For Luther, that is where reality existed by the Word of God. In contrast, a realist might say the things of creation were a reflection or representation of a greater reality beyond the senses. For Luther, there is no other greater (or allegorical) meaning that is behind the simple meaning of day and evening.

Another nominalistic tendency is in Luther's constant return to the particular – Scripture itself – rather than some overarching principle found outside or alongside Scripture. It is the Word of God that establishes reality. In his commitment to the authority of Scripture Luther follows the lead of Gabriel Biel, who some have called Luther's spiritual and theological grandfather. According to medieval scholar Heiko Oberman, Biel believed that "as the authority of the Bible does not arise from its own content but is derived from a higher authority, there is no incentive for biblical criticism, nor any possibility to be selective in one's acceptance of the biblical record. The beginning of faith is, therefore, assent to the veracity of the Christian faith, that is, assent to the Bible in its entirety."[34] Luther grasped this concept wholeheartedly, but took it further than Biel. For Luther, the Word of God was *active* in establishing reality. More than "assent" was necessary, faith was vital, for Scripture contained the very promises of God (i.e., His Word) upon which everything rested – especially, for Luther, the promise of righteousness in Christ apart from works given as a gift of God by faith. As Paul Althaus point outs, "a comparison of this aspect of Luther's work with the great theological works of scholasticism reveals the new and characteristic thrust which dominates Luther's theological method. There is no precedent for the way in which Luther, as an exegete and as a preacher, thinks in constant conversation with Scripture. Almost every single step in his theology receives its basis and direction from Scripture."[35] In a sense, Luther both incorporated late medieval nominalist principles and freed himself from them in his use and commitment to Scripture. Overall, it shows his ability to adapt and integrate the best of critical thought and methods – provided they remain subordinate to Scripture. He, in fact, also reflected a hierarchy of *faith* over *reason* much more like the realist stance of Augustine. *Faith*, based upon the Word of God (in its various forms), is primary and *reason* is valuable but secondary.

Finding Order in Creation

Order and Reason

One aspect of order Luther finds in the creation story is in the significance of the Word of God in creation. For Luther, creation always returns to, is limited by, is caused through, and held together by the Word of God. An example of this is found in a discussion of the permanence of the world and the misconception of philosophers as to the explanation for its permanence. Luther states, "But what the philosophers do not know is that this permanence is entirely the result of the power of the Word of God."[36] The Word of God seems to be quite inclusive for Luther, to draw reference to the spoken Word (as in the creation account), the written Word (as in the words of Moses – Scripture), as well as hinting at the Living Word, Jesus Christ (by Whom all things hold together – Colossians 1:17). This observation also underscores his commitment to Scriptural authority and his Christocentric theology.

Luther directly discusses the matter of order, and man's inability to grasp God's order, in the conclusion of his comments concerning the second day of creation:

> How can we understand the order to which God has given His approval? Reason must become perplexed, because what is order for God we judge to be a confusion of order. Thus because the bright stars are mixed with the less bright, the smaller with the larger, they appear planlessly mingled. Who would say that this is order? Yet there is supreme order,

established by the wisest mind... But all these instances prove that God has order and that His interpretation of order is different from ours.[37]

With this he denies the Thomist assumption that order can be grasped by reason without faith, even if that reason is redeemed. Order is ultimately defined and established by God alone, and faith is the only avenue to gain an understanding of that order.

In fact, Luther is even more direct about the subservient role of reason in grasping the mysteries and knowledge of God. In his discussion concerning the creation of the stars, he writes,

> I am nevertheless aware that human reason is far too inadequate to be able to gain a perfect knowledge of these matters. For this reason the greatest minds, overwhelmed by the grandeur of these creatures, were unable to reach any other conclusion than that they are eternal and, as it were, some sort of deities. But whereas the philosophers assert that a star is a denser part of its orb, we assert with much greater certainty that it is a light created by God through His Word.[38]

This matter-of-fact approach returns to the necessity of faith to comprehend God and the authority of His Word. Faith operates over and above reason (revealing a nominalist emphasis on faith), yet Luther never fully rejected the value of reason as long as it was subservient to faith (revealing a realist perspective on the value of reason). Without faith, natural theology and reason lead to empty speculation, which remains just that – speculation. Faith leads to a certainty that there was a plan and purpose in the mind of God for all of creation, ordered and directed by Him regardless of man's ability to comprehend it.

Order Found in the Creation of Man and Woman

An even more significant passage related to Luther's conviction of God's order as found in creation is at the beginning of his comments about God creating man and woman. It is important enough to quote the entire passage:

> Therefore let us learn that true wisdom is in Holy Scripture and in the Word of God. This gives information not only about the matter of the entire creation, not only about its form, but also about the efficient and final cause, about the beginning and about the end of all things, about who did the creating and for what purpose He created. Without the knowledge of these two causes our wisdom does not differ much from the beasts, which also make use of their eyes and ears but are utterly without the knowledge about their beginning and their end.
>
> Therefore this is an outstanding text. The more it seems to conflict with all experience and reason, the more carefully must it be noted and the more surely believed. Here we are taught about the beginning of man that the first man did not come into existence by process of generation, as reason has deceived Aristotle and the rest of the philosophers into imagining. The reproduction of his descendants takes place through procreation; but the first male was formed and created from a clod of the field, and the first female from the rib of the sleeping man. Here, therefore, we find the beginning which it is impossible to find through Aristotle's philosophy.[39]

Note Luther's reference once again to the Word of God, which forms the basis for the order that is found in creation. Also, it is clear that Luther finds order here that supercedes any consideration of the philosophers. It is beyond all experience and reason. This shows another area of influence on Luther from his nominalistic background. Faith, as the avenue for all spiritual knowledge, stands above reason as its master. By faith one must fear, love and trust God even when reason cannot comprehend or find the solution.

Matter, form, and *efficient and final cause* are philosophical terms that Luther uses and redefines not in philosophical speculation, but only as evidenced in the story of creation as revealed in Scripture through the Word of God. This is the place in which Augustine's influence is once again seen in Luther's thought. Note the similarity in Luther's *matter, form and efficient cause* and Augustine's use of *measure, form and order* (quoted earlier). It is quite interesting that Luther parallels "efficient and final cause" with Augustine's "order," and establishes a connection between God as the causer (i.e., the One who orders) and creation as the caused (i.e., that which is ordered). Although Augustine was using his terms in a much more distinctive philosophical approach, Luther draws the concept into his treatment of creation and, in typical fashion, brings the light of the Word to bear on the whole idea.

Order in the Image of God in Man

Order is found, as well, in the makeup of man as a being and the purpose for which man was created. That man was created in the image of God is an important theme in Luther's treatment of man's creation. Man stands out from the beasts, though similar in body, with the unique image that indicates "another and better life than the physical."[40] The image, however, is lost through sin and there is difficulty understanding it to any great extent.[41] Nevertheless in this weakened, sinful state there remains a difference between man and beast.[42] Scripture clearly points to the image and likeness of God in man, therefore "in eternity...he is to live with God, and while he is here on earth, he is to preach God, thank Him, and patiently obey His Word. In this life we lay hold of this goal in ever so weak a manner; but in the future life we shall attain it fully."[43] Though Luther recognizes the full effects of sin on the image, he does not fall into the trap of denigrating the physical part of man, but sees the fullness of redemption that Christ brings working in the midst of the whole man.

The Fall and Redemption of Order

The breakdown of the created order through sin is evidenced by the loss, Luther writes, of "a most beautifully enlightened reason and a will in agreement with the Word and will of God."[44] He sees this as serious, but not nearly so as that of man willfully turning away from God. Luther observes that we are unable to recognize the enormity of our loss unless we consider "that image of the state of innocence – whatever its nature may have been – in which the will was upright, and the reason was sound. Furthermore, there was the greatest dignity of the human body. When, in contrast, we reflect on the deprivation or loss of these gifts, then, in some measure, we can appraise the evil of original sin."[45] Man now actively pursues his own agenda, not God's. Reason is hostile to God, and even the most respectable will is opposed to Him. A significant consequence of this is that man hates God's Word.[46] Sin has destroyed God's order and the reflection of His image in man.

Redemption in Jesus Christ is Luther's answer to the restoration of the divine order. He clearly sees Scripture indicating this, especially in his study of Romans. An in-depth consideration of this aspect of Luther's theology is outside the bounds of this chapter, but suffice it to say that the restoration of order, in Christ, is essential as God returns His creation to its original glory, especially man who Luther describes as "the last and most beautiful work of God."[47] Having discovered a foundation for order in these first few chapters of Genesis, Luther sees redemption in Christ re-establishing that order.

Thus it can be seen how Luther finds in creation an order established and ordained by God. Although he draws from an education in late medieval scholasticism and nominalism, as well as a significant influence from the writings of Augustine and realism, he clearly allows the biblical material to mold his theology of creation and understanding of God's creative work, and breaks new hermeneutical ground in his constant reliance upon Scripture, rather than the speculative forms of philosophy evident in scholasticism. Order, in Luther's mind, is found in God's creation, damaged by man's sin and redeemed in Christ.

Parallels and Connections – the Order of Music

There are many parallels and connecting threads of thought that can be drawn between Luther's theology of creation and his theology of music. Not only in the evidence of order in both, but also based upon a larger view of what could be called Luther's worldview. His theological foundations were deep and his insights were broad as he viewed Scripture and God's activity among men through His Word and through the filter of his own thinking. God prepared Martin Luther for a unique task in history that he was uniquely qualified to fulfill, and he did so with conviction and determination in such a way that Christian thought is still affected today.

In many ways our current discussion always returns to the matter of *order*. For Luther, the evidence of order in the world was a comfort that showed God's providential care and gave hope for the final redemption of all creation in Christ. In the disorder that swirled around him personally, and the chaos that had been created by Papal misappropriation of, and claim to, divine authority, the evidence of order in theology and in music was a healing salve. Music, it seems, was the emotional expression of the joy he found in his theology. It is no wonder that the two – theology and music – are so integrally related in Luther's thought.[48]

Perhaps one can find that music, as a joyous expression of order, also inherently expresses Luther's concept of the "joyous exchange" – that Christ has taken the sinner's sin to the cross and exchanged it for His own righteousness, thus making man righteous before God. In this exchange, order was redeemed in Christ as well, especially in the re-establishment of the relationship between God and His most glorious creature – man. Whereas music is a thoroughly ordered creative art, Luther's theological and artistic sensitivities drew theology and music together naturally. They were both examples of God's redemptive order. When the gospel message (the "joyous exchange") was integrated with beautiful music, the impact was powerful.

Creation was ordered and established by God. For Luther, music was the best example of this created order. Structure and organization are inherent in creation, just as they are in music.

Theodore Hoelty-Nickel describes the relationship between created order and music in this way:

> What is music? Not only sound, not only movement, not only rhythm, not only pitch, not just the change of all these in various combinations and varieties. We have samples of music, so called, that would qualify for all and sundry aspects. What the common man misses in these and the expert decries in such noise is the lack of order of system. We can say that music is *order*. What the philosophers since Plato have said about music is that it is order, in fact, part of a divine or created order. Plato's interest is ethical and pedagogical. The order of the cosmos is reflected in the music. The Pythagorean concept of number is found in Plato's concept of music as order. This aspect of music certainly is generally appreciated today. There is an interesting line which can be drawn from Plato or Pythagoras to modern physicists who find a cosmic formula in numbers. Even the atheist Russell said that if there were a God, he would be a mathematician. Soehngen asserts that a modern scientist, Hesienberg, has found a mathematical 'Weltformel.' We would say that we can see in physical laws and in the mathematical or logical rules that govern our creation an order, created by God together with all other ruling laws. Not only *together with* but *integrated into* all the cosmos is the order of numbers and music. Bach knew it and expressed it both in his almost supernatural application of the order of music and his application of a hidden number code in his works.[49]

Luther's thoughts in drawing together the creativity of God in creation and man's ability to demonstrate that creativity in music has influenced musical endeavor ever since. This influence showed itself not only in the genius of Bach's musical legacy, but also in the following centuries of creative activity coming from the German people.

Music was so vital and important for Luther because it represented both order and freedom in perfect balance.[50] The order of properly associated rhythms, notes and melody along with the creative freedom of the composer to explore the possibilities of all elements of musical and lyrical composition could also be seen as a reflection of the balanced Christian life. Once order has been restored to man in the redemption of Christ, freedom becomes a reality in this life. In other words, freedom from sin is the result of being ordered by God and His Word. This freedom, to Luther, sets the Christian free to serve God and his neighbor out of a thankful and secure heart. One no longer needs to worry about gaining God's favor for salvation, for it is secure in the work of Christ (the "joyous exchange"). The believer can truly focus on loving his neighbor by freely giving of himself. Music reflects this freedom by serving not only as a vehicle for the Word of God and the spiritual benefit of the believer, but Luther recognized that music itself was a comfort in times of sorrow and could provide laughter in times of joy. Music provided freedom even in the midst of constraining circumstances (in which Luther found himself numerous times), as attested to by the singing of praises that Paul and Silas did while in jail (Acts 16).

The concept of order in creation, and then as found in music, creates a connection for Luther that is like the interlocking pieces of a puzzle. God's created order, as discovered and described by Luther in his commentary on Genesis chapters one through three, forms the foundation upon which Luther builds his theology of music. To interpret Luther's views on music without this basis would be to miss the point altogether. In Luther's mind, next to theology, music was the greatest evidence of God's created order. Theology and music are like the two legs upon which man's understanding of God and His Word stands. Though the other arts are important, music alone carries God's Word to men's hearts in powerful and significant ways. Charles Garside summarizes this thought by writing, "Music is to be reverenced, nothing less, because it is an agent for the transmission of the Word of God to man. The Word communicates itself by itself, to be sure, but it may be communicated as well through music. As a means of communication, therefore, music is possessed both of theological dimension and theological power."[51]

Luther's Grasp of the Big Picture

The broadness and balance of Luther's approach to theology shows his ability to grasp the "big picture" unlike most other theologians. Today this concept is referred to as "worldview." Luther's worldview was shaped by his understanding of the creation account, the fall of man into sin, and the ultimate redemption of creation and mankind in the work of Jesus Christ. As discussed earlier, he was able to break with many of the preconceptions of late medieval thought and its reliance upon philosophical systems. He then forged new ground in his unrelenting reliance upon Scripture and formulated a well-balanced biblical conception of theology that still has implications today.

Although no systematizer of theology, Luther saw the value of theological development – even of his own views – and allowed this to take place in the thought and writings of his colleague and successor, Philip Melancthon.[52] Melancthon produced, in the *Loci Communes,* a systematic theology based upon the ecumenical creeds that Luther both accepted and recommended. Not only did Luther lay a solid foundation for the Reformation, but he also allowed for continued progress and development of a theology built upon that foundation. The parallel in this is striking – Luther opened his arms to music and the arts as evidence of God's order, and also opened his arms to theological development in the same way. Development in both arenas was no threat, but showed God's creative work and its imbedded order. Continued development and refinement allowed man to discover that order and gain a deeper understanding of God and His Word.

In his theology of music, Luther also sought to balance an adherence to the historical creeds and the theology of Augustine with an allowance for continued musical development. There are instances in which he expects and desires those of greater ability to continue to develop the musical heritage of the church. As Paul Henry Lang pointed out, "Thus, although the fundamental idea in Luther's mind was to arrange his music for the sake of what he called the 'common ordinary man,' he endeavored to leave the door open for a possible artistic development. This remarkable man realized that a one-sided, popular, and earth-bound movement in art must inevitably decline."[53] Germany's long list of great composers is a testament to Luther's open arms of acceptance and "big picture" view of music as a gift of God reflecting His image in man. He was not threatened by the contribution of others, nor their creative activity – especially as it had been redeemed by Christ. The redemption of this art exemplifies a return to the order of creation unlike any other.

Given Luther's familiarity with the technical aspects of music, as well as his apparent abilities and gifts in performing and composing, there is little doubt that he saw the entire redemptive story (creation, fall and redemption) inherent within this great gift of God. He noted the reflection of creation in the order and structure of the music itself. He may have also recognized a representation of the fall in the dissonant aspects of music, which add tension and disharmony to it and cry for resolution (i.e., redemption?). Undoubtedly, Luther's heart and soul responded exuberantly to the redemptive aspect of music as it resolved tension and became a thing of beauty – lifting the heart and soul toward heaven – as does the redemptive work of Christ. The story of creation, fall and redemption, as broad categories of theology, also find their place in God's beautiful gift of music.

Chapter 4

Luther's Theology in Context

Martin Luther influenced the church's worship in so many ways that literally volumes of material have been written and collected in regard to his views on the subject. John Calvin, as well, had an important part in the development of a musical heritage within the Reformation. Both were quite deliberate in the formulation and communication of their views, and music is by far the most significant part of worship which both unites and separates Luther and Calvin – as well as the resultant development of the Lutheran and Reformed traditions. Huldrych Zwingli, the third of the major reformers, also formed a theology of music, but one which was both extreme and exclusive.

First to consider in this chapter will be some similarities between Luther and Calvin's thought concerning music that form a basis from which these Reformers establish their views. This will include a short synopsis of Zwingli's extreme view as well. The second consideration will be to note the differences between Luther and Calvin, which then shape their use of music in the church.

Some Similarities Between Luther and Calvin

Worship in the Vernacular

There was much in common between Luther and Calvin as they sought to refine and reform worship in their time. This section will focus on four of the most important areas of similarity: the use of the vernacular; music as the gift of God; communication of the Word; and the attitude of the heart.

Of the greatest importance for both of them was that elements of worship should take place in the vernacular – the language of the common people. This was evident in the hymnals used in their churches, which were developed and printed for the people. Luther, in a letter to Spalatin in 1524, said, "[Our] plan is to follow the example of the prophets and the ancient fathers of the church, and to compose psalms for the people [in the] vernacular, that is, spiritual songs, so that the Word of God may be among the people also in the form of music."[54] Although Luther allowed other parts of the service to remain in Latin, he felt that significant portions of it – including the readings of the Word, the sermon, and the singing – should be in the vernacular in order to make it accessible to the people. Peter Auksi notes, "Luther's most distinctive contribution to the reform of liturgy, a contribution which Zwingli keenly appreciated and promoted, was to re-emphasize the role of the word, the sermon, in worship. In vernacular homilies the faithful could be taught the means of fostering and safeguarding their belief and a correct understanding of the action celebrated in the Mass."[55]

Calvin also held this conviction and saw to it that *every* part of worship was in the vernacular. He said, "...public prayers must be couched not in Greek among the Latins, nor in Latin among the French or English, as has heretofore been the custom, but in the language of the people, which can be generally understood by the whole assembly. For this ought to be done for the edification of the whole church, which receives no benefit whatever from a sound not understood."[56] He saw this, as did Luther, facilitating the communication of the Word into the life of the people both within the formal worship of the church, as well as within their lives at home.

Music as the Gift of God

Music as the gift of God was also important for both Luther and Calvin. Luther was unabashedly positive in his commendation of music. His most cogent comments on worship are found in the prefaces to hymnals and other collections of music. In the *Preface to Georg Rhau's Symphoniea Iucundae of 1538* he writes,

Here it must suffice to discuss the benefit of this great art. But even that transcends the greatest eloquence of the most eloquent, because of the infinite variety of its forms and benefits. We can mention only one point (which experience confirms), namely, that next to the Word of God, music deserves the highest praise...After all, the gift of language combined with the gift of song was only given to man to let him know that he should praise God with both word and music, namely, by proclaiming (the Word of God) through music and by providing sweet melodies with words.[57]

Here we find Luther lauding the "forms and benefits" of music as part of the Christian life, which, as previously noted, parallel the themes of theology – especially in reflecting the pattern of creation, fall and redemption. But he also saw the benefits of theology as music reflected the "joyous exchange" and the active nature of the Word of God.

Calvin, on the other hand, was somewhat more reserved. He also recognized that music was a gift bestowed by God, for he wrote, "Now among the other things proper to recreate man and give him pleasure, music is either the first or one of the principal, and we must think that it is a gift of God deputed to that purpose."[58] Charles Garside notes that it is apparent that Calvin's commitment to music as used in worship grew as his theology grew. He was quite reserved (approaching Zwingli's extreme view of allowing no music in worship) in his views prior to his exile from Geneva (in 1538) to Strasbourg, but by the time he returned to Geneva (in 1541) he had developed a deep commitment to and recognition of the value of music for worship. It is quite interesting that evidence points to a German (Lutheran) congregation in Strasbourg, under the leadership of Martin Bucer, which influenced Calvin's view on music in the church because of his experience there in hearing that congregation sing.[59] In this manner Luther seems to have influenced Calvin, through the Strasbourg congregation, away from the extreme of Zwingli and toward a more moderate, inclusive (though limited) view of music as a gift of God, and its utility for the people of God.

Communicating the Word of God

As Reformers, Luther and Calvin had the common goal of challenging the Catholic Church in its abuses – and the area of music was no exception. Both found there to be too much distraction in the way the Catholic Church allowed either inappropriate musical adornment, which distracted from the lyric, or obvious theological problems in the lyrics themselves. They both agreed that the emphasis should be upon the communication of the Word of God. Music could be used as a vehicle to deliver the Word, as long as it did not confuse, cover or distract from that Word. In the *Preface to the Babst Hymnal of 1545*, Luther penned this short poem:

> *A Warning by D. Martin Luther:*
> Many false masters now hymns indite
> Be on your guard and judge them aright.
> Where God is building his church and word,
> There comes the devil with lie and sword.[60]

Luther's point is obvious – the music of the hymns must not be allowed to hide a false doctrine in the lyrics. He is clear in this objective as he allows the use of even Catholic music in his churches, with careful alterations to the texts:

> And indeed, they also possess a lot of splendid, beautiful songs and music, especially in the cathedral and parish churches. But these are used to adorn all sorts of impure and idolatrous texts. Therefore, we have unclothed these idolatrous, lifeless, and foolish texts, and divested them of their beautiful music. We have put this music on the living and holy Word of God in order to sing, praise, and honor it. We want the beautiful art of music to be properly used to serve her dear Creator and his Christians. He is thereby praised and honored

and we are made better and stronger in faith when his holy Word is impressed on our hearts by sweet music.[61]

For Calvin, simplicity was the chief concern in the communication of the Word, and the Catholic use of music was anything but simple. He desired to keep the Word pure, in order for it to communicate most effectively. Auksi comments, "Because Calvin sees material images and 'idols' as dominant in Catholic worship, the problem of idolatry again becomes a major issue both in the *Institutes* and in Calvinism internationally. Not only do images lure a Christian into a religion of the senses, but they also invite the distracted worshipper to give spiritual attention to something other than God, who in Calvin's conception is a magnificently transcendent being utterly beyond all imagery, picturing, and crass visualization."[62] In light of these abuses of the Catholic Church, Calvin sought to remove distractions, especially of the senses, from worship.

The role of the Word as central to worship is apparent in the thought of both men by the centrality of the sermon in their liturgies, as well as the overall emphasis on biblical integrity throughout their theological discourses. It is no surprise that this same commitment would find its way into the use of music as well. Though Luther's reforms precede Calvin's by several years, this is an indication that there is a general agreement in the broader Reformation of the areas needing reform.

The Attitude of the Heart

The attitude of the heart was also of great common concern to Luther and Calvin. For both, a right heart before God was more important than the beauty of any music. Luther thought to use music as a guide – to help establish proper modes of thinking. For example, Christian music is for "the young – who should at any rate be trained in music and other fine arts – something to wean them away from love ballads and carnal songs and to teach them something of value in their place, thus combining the good with the pleasing, as is proper for youth."[63] This was a very utilitarian usage of music as a vehicle for truth.

Calvin, seeking a more careful approach, warned against the possibility of the music itself becoming a distraction from the message. He writes:

> And surely, if the singing be tempered to that gravity which is fitting in the sight of God and the angels, it both lends dignity and grace to sacred actions and has the greatest value in kindling our hearts to a true zeal and eagerness to pray. Yet we should be very careful that our ears be not more attentive to the melody than our minds to the spiritual meaning of the words...On the other hand, such songs as have been composed only for sweetness and delight of the ear are unbecoming to the majesty of the church and cannot but displease God in the highest degree.[64]

This focus upon the attitude of the heart, though approached in varying ways, is a common factor in the Reformers' insistence upon spiritual worship. How this worked out in real life is what led to significant differences in the way the Lutheran and Reformed traditions ultimately practiced worship. Luther, with his emphasis on faith, certainly saw the heart attitude as an important aspect of the Christian life. The praise of God must spring forth from a thankful heart, just as good works spring forth from thankfulness for God's provision of salvation by faith in Jesus Christ.

The View of Zwingli

In stark contrast to Luther, and even narrower than Calvin were the views of Huldrych Zwingli. Zwingli basically omitted music as a whole from the liturgy. Charles Garside, in his valuable work titled *Zwingli and the Arts*, summarizes this point by noting that according to Zwingli, liturgical music was "scripturally indefensible on three closely interrelated, yet distinguishable, grounds:

1) Music in worship is not explicitly commanded by God in either the Old or New Testament.
2) Christ instructed men to pray to God individually and in private. (John 4:24)
3) Saint Paul urged men, when together, to worship God and pray to Him in their hearts. (Colossians 3:16)[65]

Zwingli's focus on prayer as the purest from of worship dominated his view of liturgical forms, and to him, prayer by its very nature was internal and private. The liturgy was simple and straightforward. Donald Hustad describes it by writing, "Zwinglian liturgy tended to be more didactic than devotional. His typical morning service resembled the ancient Prone liturgy, consisting of Scripture reading (Epistle and Gospel), preaching, and a long prayer."[66] This was seen as a pure Pauline form of worship. Music simply had no place, even in the Calvinistic idea that singing the Psalms could be considered "sung prayer."

This view of worship led to a sharp distinction between what Zwingli thought to be "true worship" (private, individual prayer), and the "hypocritical liturgy" (public, external show) of the Catholic Church. "The choral and instrumental music of the contemporary Catholic Church was full of the repetition of many words. Furthermore, it had become increasingly a matter of display before men, frequently a dazzling display of the technical abilities not only of the performer, but of the composer."[67] Zwingli sought for pure worship in focusing and communicating with God in prayer. He writes, "...for whenever the human heart is truly intent on communicating with God it prefers to be alone, as Christ well knew. Therefore He pointed to a quiet place in which one could speak with the heavenly Father."[68] Garside comments on this statement:

> With that [summary] Zwingli reveals the extremity of his reach. What he seeks is nothing less than an irreducible purity of worship – in other words, an absolutely private prayer: the individual withdrawn from the world and from his fellow men,

absolutely alone in communion with his heavenly Father. The Father's Son has commanded such worship. Therefore, ideally, no other form should be considered, for no other form would accord so literally with the law of Christ. Thus Christ's instructions stand at the very core of Zwingli's liturgical thinking, for out of which all else radiates and without which the external form in which his liturgy was finally cast cannot be comprehended...

Such an ideal could scarcely be realized, however, if the communal worship of the visible Church is to be observed and retained, and this for Zwingli was a necessity beyond dispute. The content of prayer must be given some formal, ritual expression in public. Yet once worship is made public, full opportunity is immediately provided for countless varieties of hypocrisy and display.[69]

Interestingly enough, Zwingli himself was a very accomplished musician and could play virtually any instrument he desired, and did so – outside of the church and its worship. His personal theology simply would not allow the use of music in the church, and to that conviction he was true. So true that he even had the organs in the cathedrals of Zurich removed and destroyed!

Another factor to consider, especially for the purpose of this study, is how Zwingli's view of creation may have affected his view of music. In his educational background, as W.P. Stephens writes, "it seems clear that his studies at Basle (1502-6) acquainted him with the *via antiqua* [i.e. realism] and the *via moderna* [i.e., nominalism], although the former almost certainly predominated...Moreover Zwingli's library is evidence of his reading of Aquinas and Duns Scotus."[70] This clearly led to presuppositional differences between Zwingli's approach and Luther's. Stephens continues:

Some of the differences between them [Luther and Zwingli] could be expected from differences in their background, although the one does not necessarily lead to the other. Their different scholastic education is one factor that could naturally lead them to different presuppositions in theology and Zwinlgi's Erasmian heritage could do the same. Their different experience of the priesthood (Zwingli as a parish priest and army chaplain, Luther as a monk) could naturally provoke Zwingli to a theology more concerned with society as a whole and Luther to one more concerned with the individual. The different political and social contexts of their ministry, with Zwingli needing the support of a council and not simply that of one man, could naturally stimulate him to have a different understanding of ministry and to engage in it in a different way.[71]

More significantly, Zwingli's view of the creation of man sheds light on this subject. In *On the Providence of God* he writes that man "was, therefore, given a body as he was marked out to be the chief of all bodily beings, and he was given a soul, as he alone of all bodily creatures was to have kinship and fellowship with God and all other spiritual beings – a body and a soul, two most widely different things. For what differs more widely from the clearness and light of the mind and intelligence than the dull inactivity of the earth and the body?"[72] It is clear that Zwingli has a very low regard for the physical part of creation, and in fact denigrates it. Obviously, anything that would correlate to the physical and the senses, even music as a sense-filled experience, was unworthy to be part of the contemplation and consideration of God. The following quote both summarizes and helps one visualize Zwingli's concept of the differences between the physical and spiritual parts of man:

> So it is with man. His mind is a clear, limpid stream, flowing forth from the Godhead itself. Hence it is so eager for truth and right and so devoted to them that if you could consider it apart from the dull mass of the body, as the angels are, you would detect nothing base, disturbing, or defiling in it. The body is clay, taken from the earth, and when you attach this to the soul it is like letting a wild boar into a liquid spring. Thus what the soul by itself would see clearly and would follow readily and without hesitation, it now sees dimly, on account of the

grossness of the clay being like a mist upon it, and is held bound by the weight of that clay as by fetters, so that it can no more pursue the perfect course than Tantalus could seize its fruit. Hence that sort of internal war in which the mind and the body are engaged against each other. When the mind begins to contemplate God, to talk and commune with Him about the things it has in common with Him, suddenly the flesh, fashioned from clay, draws it back. 'Fool,' it cries, 'Where are you going? There is no Deity; much less one that cares for our affairs.' Thus each part of man constantly looks back upon its origin. The mind yearns for light, purity and goodness, inasmuch as its nature is light, its substance pure and devoted to the right, seeing that it derives its origin from the Godhead; the body inclines to idleness, laziness, darkness and dullness, as it is lazy and indolent by nature, and without reason and intelligence, seeing that it consists of earth.[73]

With this understanding of Zwingli's extreme and exclusive views of music and the arts, as well as his low opinion of the physical creation, one can see the striking difference between Zwingli and the other Reformers, but especially Luther, and how Luther has had a much more positive impact on the church in this area throughout the centuries. The remainder of this chapter will return now to the views of Luther and Calvin as representative of the broader Reformation influence on the use of music in liturgy and worship.

Some Differences Between Luther and Calvin

One hears of the distinctive differences between the Reformers much more often than the similarities primarily because it is the area of worship between the Lutheran and Reformed traditions in which one sees these differences, and the outward appearance in styles of worship is easily noticed even for those who are unaware of the reasons behind them. The basis of these differences is found in Luther's and Calvin's differing emphasis on Scripture, but it does not stop there – they both appeal to Augustine for their particular view. One can also find differences in what they each say concerning the inclusion/exclusion of various texts, as well as the inclusion/exclusion of particular musical structures or styles. These differences also stem from a fundamental difference in the way that these two men viewed the physical part of the creation of man.

The Appeal to Scripture

Both Luther and Calvin appeal to Scripture as the basis for their view of music. According to Auksi, "The strident demands for conformity to new ceremonies, however purified, in Luther's eyes threatened a new legalism, particularly since directions for public worship in the New Testament represented at best a direction or emphasis, not a command."[74] The interpretation of the Scriptural text as bestowing a sense of "direction" allowed a quite open view for the inclusion of all types of music for Luther, and significantly set him apart from Calvin. Luther draws from a wide collection of biblical references in explaining his view of the use of music:

> Every Christian knows that the practice of singing spiritual songs is wholesome and well-pleasing unto God, for everybody knows that not only the prophets and kings of Israel (who praised God with vocal and instrumental music, with songs and stringed instruments), but also the early Christians, who sang especially psalms, used music already in the early stages of the Church's history. Indeed, St. Paul encouraged the use of music (1 Cor 14) and in his Epistle to the Colossians he insists that Christians appear before God with psalms and spiritual songs which emanate from the heart, in order that through these the Word of God and Christian doctrine may be preached, taught, and put into practice.[75]

Luther, in effect, opens his arms to music and molds it to the service of the Word of God.

Calvin's followers avoid embracing Luther's championing of art due to Calvin's interpretation of John 4:24, especially for personal use or within the liturgy. In his comments on John 4:24, Calvin called the church to "remove the coverings of the ancient ceremonies and retain what is spiritual in the worship of God. For the truth of the worship of God rests in the Spirit, and ceremonies are so to say adventitious."[76] This is, for Calvin, the "pure and simple substance of spiritual worship,"[77] and it is what sets Luther and Calvin apart. Calvin focuses upon Christ's definition of worship in John 4:24 and allows that to be the central hub from which he builds the rest of his theology of music. This view is right in line with Zwingli, who viewed worship primarily as prayer, which is an inward work of God. Externals (i.e., music, sculpture, visual art) in true worship are not only unnecessary, but also unwanted. Garside notes that Calvin "well understood Zwingli's concern for the capacity of music to distract from prayer, and shared Zwingli's fear that the congregation would merely delight in singing, rather than delight in worshiping through song. Inevitably he would regard the musical splendour of the Lutheran liturgy as too distracting."[78] Calvin does not go to Zwingli's extreme of eliminating music entirely and allows music to be used in facilitating the praise of God and prayers to Him, but that with great limitations. He says in his *Letter to the Reader* in the Geneva Psalter of 1542, "Now there are in brief three things that our Lord has commanded us to observe in our spiritual assemblies, namely, the preaching of His word, the public and solemn prayers, and the administration of His sacraments... As to the public prayers, these are of two kinds: some are offered by means of words alone, the other with song."[79]

This shows Calvin's distrust of the senses and the physical stemming from his view that the body was the "prison-house" of the soul. He writes, "Christ commended His spirit to His Father, and Stephen commended his spirit to Christ, meaning that when the soul is released from the prison-house of the body God is its constant guardian."[80] Like Zwingli, Calvin has a "lower view" of the physical part of creation than that of Luther and considers the internal relationship as the only true focus for spiritual things. It is apparent that this is a significant difference compared to Luther, who could be considered as having a "higher view" of creation that allowed for physical manifestations of the internal working of God's Spirit. The internal was still of primary importance to Luther, but his view of man's body as a good part of creation gave him the understanding that man was a physical-spiritual integrated being.

To show Calvin's lower view of creation, and of man's body in particular, note the interplay between the positive, internal aspects of man and the negative, physical aspects in this quote:

> Finally, the many splendid faculties which the mind possesses, crying out that it bears the stamp of divinity, are so many proofs of its immortal and personal existence. For the sense possessed by the brutes goes no further than the body, or at the most extends to objects with which they meet; but the activity of the human mind traverses heaven and earth, penetrates the secrets of nature, comprehends and remembers the course of ages, and infers things future from things that are past, clearly proving that something separate from the body lies hidden within man.[81]

This lower view of creation becomes even clearer as Calvin seeks to distinguish the difference between man as a created being and the rest of the created animal kingdom. The difference is the internal and spiritual. The physical body is basically the same as that of the "brutes." He explains:

> A solid proof of the existence of the soul is supplied by the statement that man was made in the image of God; for though the glory of the Creator shines in the external form of man, it is certain that the seat of the divine image is in the soul. It is true that our outward appearance, distinguishing us from the brutes, shows that we are nearer to God than they. Nor do I object to the opinion that the words "in the image of God" refer in part to the dignity of the human form. Even a heathen poet has said (Ovid, *Metamorphoses*, I 84-86):

> *Brutes eye the ground: to man alone 'tis given*
> *To lift his head and scan the vault of heaven.*
> Yet it must not be forgotten that the image of God which is indicated by these outward marks is a spiritual character. It consists in the integrity with which Adam was endowed when he possessed a right understanding, affections subject to sound reason, and senses under perfect and orderly control.[82]

Note in the final sentence that Calvin reiterates the medieval concept of the "rightly ordered man," who controls the physical and sensual by understanding and sound reason. He sees this concept as part of the original creation.

Luther and Calvin, then, differ in their views of creation. These can be designated "higher" and "lower" respectively. This does not mean that Calvin sees no good in creation, but it probably denotes a continuing struggle between his study of Scripture and his neo-Platonic background. Nor does one want to assume that Luther sees a physical creation without serious limitations. The difference is, as both men seek balance, Calvin leans on the side of a "lower view" and Luther toward a "higher view" of God's creation. This allows Luther a greater degree of freedom in recognizing the gift of music as part of God's created order.

The Appeal to Augustine

During the Reformation, Augustine was a favorite for everyone to support their views on varieties of issues, and the Reformers quoted him often. In his *Confessions*, Augustine writes:

> Thus I fluctuate between the danger of pleasure and the experience of the beneficent effect, and I am more led to put forward the opinion (not as an irrevocable view) that the custom of singing in Church is to be approved, so that through the delights of the ear the weaker mind may rise up towards the devotion of worship. Yet when it happens to me that the music moves me more than the subject of the song, I confess myself to

commit a sin deserving punishment, and then I would prefer not to have heard the singer.[83]

Luther reads this and views it in the best possible light: "Music is a beautiful and lovely gift of God which has often moved and inspired me to preach with joy. St. Augustine was afflicted with scruples of conscience whenever he discovered that he had derived pleasure from music and had been made happy thereby; he was of the opinion that such joy is unrighteous and sinful. He was a fine pious man; however, if he were living today, he would hold with us..."[84] Essentially, Luther expects that Augustine would have grown in his appreciation of the utility and benefit of music. This is quite remarkable from Luther, an Augustinian monk, for as Walter Buszin remarks, "Augustinian thought was always strongly in evidence wherever music showed an arrested development, as in Italy prior to the *ars nova*, and in the Calvinistic provinces of Western Europe."[85] Luther did not allow Augustine's "scruples of conscience" to stop him from taking a very broad approach to music.

One can understand why Calvin read Augustine's words as a warning. Calvin was so concerned with protecting the purity of the heart, that he would rather remove the possibility that music could become a distraction from true worship. James Sydnor, in his study of Calvin's hymns, observes that "Calvin had the Herculean task of setting forth and safeguarding the new Reformed theology, [and thus] his concern was that any use of music should be edifying."[86] Calvin recognized the power of music to move the hearer emotionally and he fell in line with Augustine by taking his warning seriously, restricting both the use and development of music within the Reformed church tradition.

The Issue of Lyrics and Text

As far as what texts should be included in the music of the church, the Reformers differed dramatically in what Garside calls the "irreconcilable difference between Luther and Calvin over the practical question of *what* was to be sung, with respect to textual content as well as musical structure."[87] Luther again is quite inclusive, "so long as musicians and poets, separately or together, were enriching the liturgy to a 'pious use,' their imaginative faculties were unrestricted."[88] Luther's concern was for making music a useful tool in the service of God for the proclamation of the Word. In the *Preface to the Burial Hymns of 1542*, Luther explains his attitude toward using even the music of the Catholic Church:

> This is also why we have collected the fine music and songs which under the papacy were used at vigils, masses for the dead, and burials. Some fine examples of these we have printed in this booklet and we, or whoever is more gifted than we, will select more of them in the future. But we have adapted other texts to the music so that it may adorn our article of the resurrection, instead of purgatory with its torment and satisfaction which lets their dead neither sleep nor rest. The melodies and notes are precious. It would be a pity to let them perish. But the texts and words are non-Christian and absurd. They deserve to perish.[89]

Calvin, on the other hand, limits musical texts to the psalms. It is admirable that Calvin is consistent in his application of these guidelines in order to protect the purity of the worshipper's heart, which is of pre-eminent importance over and above any sensual pleasure. Once again appealing to Augustine, Calvin wrote, "Now what Saint Augustine says is true – that no one can sing things worthy of God save what he has received from Him. Wherefore, although we look far and wide and search on every hand, we shall not find better songs nor songs better suited to that end than the psalms of David which the Holy Spirit made and uttered through him."[90] The resulting outcome of this was that Calvin and his followers became psalm singers. "For Calvin both text and form existed already, ordained by God and given by Him to men so that through them they might praise Him...And as between the psalm and the hymn, Calvin definitively chose the psalm..."[91] In contrast to the freedom that Luther allowed poets and musicians, and the great wealth of music which came out of the Lutheran tradition, Calvin chose a conservative route. He both allowed and limited the type of texts permitted in worship in one overarching principle. Garside summarizes Calvin's view by explaining, "The theological grounds which allow singing in the liturgy actually act also as a principle of restriction on the freedom of the artist. Only the psalms of David were to be used during worship; no other texts were to be introduced. The psalms were simply to be rendered into the vernacular and versified; the function of the poet was reduced thereby to translating and re-shaping an existing text."[92]

The issue of lyrical and textual use for Calvin was restriction. For Luther it was one of freedom, which reflects the freedom of the Christian in the thankful response, by faith, to God for His mercy and provision of righteousness in Christ.

Musical Structure and Style

The difference between Luther and Calvin is just as stark in the area of musical structure and style. Luther is open to the fullness of man's creativity, but Calvin would limit the music itself, as well as its development, demonstrating another example of Calvin's "lower view" of creation in comparison with Luther's "higher view." This is quite apparent in the way they produced and edited the songbooks for their churches. As Garside points out, "Whereas the Genevan Psalter of 1562 is, in effect, the work of only three men, the poets Clement Marot and Theodore de Beze, and the musician Loys Bourgeoys, working under the unremitting superintendency of Calvin, the Lutheran *Erfurter Enchiridion* of 1524, for example, is a collection, extensive and various, not only of translation and revisions of Latin and German hymns, but of folk songs, both German and Latin, as well. The *Enchiridion*, indeed, neglects virtually none of the textual and musical expression of mediaeval piety."[93]

Luther writes, "I would certainly like to praise music with all my heart as the excellent gift of God which it is and to commend it to everyone. But I am so overwhelmed by the diversity and magnitude of its virtue and benefits that I can find neither beginning nor end or method for my discourse. As much as I want to commend it, my praise is bound to be wanting and inadequate."[94] Such was Luther's unreserved praise for music itself as a means of communicating the Word of God. He repeatedly bestows upon music the title of "gift of God," as has already been mentioned, and for Luther this attitude was undeniable in how God allowed music to affect the human soul. "Luther had openly proclaimed his desire to use all available music, including the most obviously secular, for the worship of the church. The fact that he placed so few, if any, restrictions on the music to be employed led to the creation of the so-called *contrafacta*, that is to say popular songs, whose melodies were well and widely known, adopted to liturgical use by means of new texts."[95]

Calvin's limitation upon music in the church went beyond just the text and was applied to the music as well. Rather than allowing freedom, as Luther did, the musician's function "was a subordinate one. He was compelled to limit himself simply to providing notes for the already established metre of a given psalm text. More confining yet was the stipulation that these psalms be sung by the congregation only in unison; no other musical versions were to be admitted to the worship of the Genevan Church."[96] Calvin saw the use of musical instruments as part of Israel's worship. This was supplanted by the more pure worship of the church,[97] and thereby excluded instrumentation of any kind. He also rejected any crossover between music for worship and music for pleasure, noting that the use of unaccompanied, unison psalm singing was the only music worthy of God and the angels.[98]

***

In the context of the Reformation, Luther's theology of music held elements in common with the views of other Reformers, as well as differing from them. It has been shown that Luther and Calvin held compatible views and emphasized four areas: 1) the use of music in the vernacular; 2) music as the gift of God; 3) communicating the Word of God through music was of primary importance; and 4) the importance of protecting and encouraging the proper heart attitude of the believer.

As for the differences, Zwingli's view (in this area of church life and theology) was extreme and not critical to this discussion. Luther and Calvin, as representing the broader Reformation, recognized the need for musical expression but differed in at least four areas: 1) their appeal to Scripture; 2) their appeal to Augustine; 3) on the issue of freedom for lyrics and texts; and 4) on the issue of freedom for musical structure and style.

Overall, one finds Luther's views more inclusive and balanced in comparison to the others. He was concerned about the inner man, but also sought to give freedom, with discernment, to musical (and other artistic) expression as the redeemed believer celebrated the gift of salvation and the assurance of life in Christ.

Chapter 5

A Comprehensive and Balanced View

It is perplexing that in the midst of the breadth of study that has been done on Luther and Calvin in relation to music in the church, that very few, if any, look at the broader biblical perspective by asking whether either of them struck a balance in their philosophy and use of music. This reluctance seems to be due to the fact that most of the studies simply wish to reveal the thoughts of these two men, rather than evaluate them. So these questions arise: Are either of their views comprehensive in considering all of the aspects of what the arts represent in man? Is either of their views balanced in interpretation of the biblical texts? Does either view adequately deal with personal holiness issues with which both men were concerned? This section will begin discussing these questions, but let it be stated that Luther's view seems to be much more in balance with the overall perspective of biblical theology than Calvin's, and hopefully the reasons for this conclusion will be clear.

A Comprehensive View

Is Luther's or Calvin's view comprehensive in considering all of the aspects of what the arts represent in man? The purpose of this question is two-fold: Is there recognition that Christ's work of redemption applies to the whole being of man, not just his soul? And, secondly, is there recognition of the creative arts as part of God's image found in man? It has already been stated that Luther's attitude toward the function of music, and the arts in general, has been that of open arms. Inclusiveness, tempered by a strong sense of good theology, a right heart, and subordination to the proclamation of the Word was his desire. He did not wish that "the gospel should destroy and blight all the arts, as some of the pseudo-religious claim. But [he] would

55

like to see the arts, especially music, used in the service of Him who gave them and made them."[99]

There is a real sense in which Luther approaches music with a redemptive attitude that Calvin is reluctant to consider, though he carefully acknowledges some value in it, by allowing the singing of unison Psalms. As part of God's creation, music should be returned to Him in praise, adoration and prayer. Luther would rather allow the Spirit of God to transform the music than to limit its use and as a result limit the possible transmission of the Word of God. This attitude is evident in a letter to Ludwig Senfl in 1530, in which Luther writes:

> I am not ashamed to confess publicly that next to theology there is no art which is the equal of music, for she alone, after theology, can do what otherwise only what theology can accomplish, namely, quiet and cheer up the soul of man, which is clear evidence that the devil, the originator of depressing worries and troubled thoughts, flees from the voice of music just as he flees from the words of theology. For this very reason the prophets cultivated no art so much as music in that they attached their theology not to geometry, nor to arithmetic, nor to astronomy, but to music, speaking the truth through psalms and hymns.[100]

In fact, Luther's redemptive attitude is, for him, a reflection of the work of Christ. Auksi draws this together by noting, "Luther's positive valuation of art rests on the lesson of the Incarnation. Like Augustine, he justifies music in the spiritual life on the grounds that man needs the mediation of body, matter, and the senses to grasp the immaterial. God's kindness and wisdom made the ineffable Son manifest 'by some definite and visible form which can be seen with the eyes and touched with the hands, in short, is within the scope of the five senses.'"[101] The fact that God saw fit to become man and submit Himself to the senses shows that God redeemed those senses in His Son. Likewise, since music is enjoyed by the senses, it is also redeemed by Christ's work. Luther's "higher view" of creation is evident once again and, coupled with the significance of Christ Himself humbly taking the form of man, raises the value of the human body in Luther's thought.

At an even more basic level, Brian L. Horne's observation quoted in Chapter 2 concerning Luther's view of music indicates that its foundational connection to order permeates the entirety of his theology and worldview. With this in mind, it can be inferred that Luther recognizes music as part of the image of God expressing itself in man. Again, Christ's work redeems man in his entirety, and music as part of His image in man reflects that redeeming influence. The thoroughness in which Luther examines the gift of music allows him to give balance in an extraordinary way.

Calvin, on the other hand, limited the use of music in an attempt to protect the inner man and attitude of the heart. As Nathaniel Micklem points out, for Calvin "the only acceptable worship of God is from the heart; and since this inward attitude alone determines real devotion to God and His will, worship becomes relatively independent of given forms; the outward is depreciated and dependence on it discouraged."[102] This protectionism is admirable, but does not seem to leave enough to the work of God in the hearts of men. It strikes more of a Platonic Dualism, from which Calvin often struggled to be free, than a balanced biblical theology. Calvin's attitude is admirable in recognizing that the inner man (the spirit) is more important to the spiritual life than the outer man (the material) and that the latter needs to be suppressed in whatever way is needed, but here we see more evidence of his "lower view" of creation (that is, the physical part of man) as "Calvin sternly limits his own humanism and training, preferring to restrict the free, full plan of the outward man and his senses in favour of an inward spiritual culture and a few cleansed arts, and speaking out frequently about the materializing effect of idolatrous images."[103] Calvin struggled to balance Christian freedom and restriction and tended to lean toward a restrictive, careful approach even while recognizing the goodness of God's gifts.

Luther, in contrast, allowed the idea of the redemption of Christ (the "joyous exchange") to permeate into the entirety of life – and thus to music.

Biblical Balance

As for the balance in interpretation of the biblical texts, it becomes somewhat difficult to assess in that the same texts are not necessarily used in defense of a particular position. Luther takes his cue primarily from Colossians 3:16, *"Let the word of Christ richly dwell within you, with all wisdom teaching and admonishing one another with psalms and hymns and spiritual songs, singing with thankfulness in your hearts to God."* In this verse, and others which are similar (Ephesians 5:19-20), Luther finds the Apostle Paul allowing a wide diversity of techniques in teaching the Word of God. He desires to follow Paul's example in his own view of worship, and specifically the area of music.

Calvin takes his approach primarily from John 4:24, *"God is spirit, and those who worship Him must worship in spirit and in truth."* This fits nicely with his "lower view" of creation and raises the importance of the spiritual in the worship of God, and this would apply to music as used by the church in its ceremonies. Calvin said, "What it is to worship God in Spirit and truth appears plainly from what has already been said. It is to remove the coverings of the ancient ceremonies and retain simply what is spiritual in the worship of God."[104] Here we find, again, a struggle with balance. It is, in some ways, an "either/or" scenario for Calvin rather than the "both/and" of Luther.

Determining the nature of the "spiritual" in worship is a major area where Luther and Calvin differ. Luther approaches it as inclusive, expansive and redemptive. Calvin looks at it as exclusive, limited and protective. Luther asks, "What can we use as part of the worship of God?" Calvin asks, "What must we avoid as part of the worship of God?" Luther is "willing and eager to adapt matter to spirit, while Calvin seeks to lessen the human need for sensuous stimulation in order to intensify spirit."[105] In their interpretation of the biblical texts, Luther once again strikes a balance, while Calvin seems to lean toward and teach restriction.

Personal Holiness – Freedom or Restriction?

Personal holiness (piety) was important to both of these Reformers, as was mentioned earlier, but the question remains as to whether their particular view helped or hurt the pursuit of holiness. Did freedom or restriction represent the biblical pattern more accurately? Christianity is a religion of freedom, and Luther achieved this emphasis, especially as it relates to the idea of redemption (as discussed above). Auksi observes, "Luther trusts in the individual's ability to distinguish between superfluous pomp and 'necessary ceremonies' and to use art correctly, rather than rejecting it outright from the reformed life and spirit."[106]

Paul Nettl, in his book *Luther and Music*, brings Luther's thoughts together in a well-written synopsis, specifically noting this aspect of creative freedom:

> Music, for Luther, is an expression of faith – a gift by the grace of God. He links music with the grace of God, with the experience of God, and with Christ's act of salvation. He who believes in this salvation by Christ cannot help but be happy, and sing and tell about it, so that others may hear it and come to Him. It is not so much a question of whether he can, but that he must; just as the artist *must* express his feelings in color or tones. It is the principle of artistic freedom, which corresponds to the principle of Christian liberty – a liberty which is in sharp contrast to compulsion, to law. 'Forced love offends God' is a popular proverb characterizing the compulsion of the old Church. Luther often expressed the idea that music spontaneously flowing from the inmost soul is the image of evangelical freedom, the freedom of the Christian man.[107]

Calvin, by contrast, thought more in terms of protecting the individual from having too much freedom in worldly things. He made an earnest attempt to protect the individual from the influence of the world and created a limited framework within which worship and creativity should function. Micklem notes:

> The stark simplicity of Calvinist worship was not negative at all but was an attempt to solve one of the fundamental questions concerning freedom raised by the Reformation, namely, the relation of freedom to the world. Under the new sense of the significance of freedom a new import was given to the truth that the only acceptable worship is of the heart, and that the intrusion of the merely material attraction is a degradation of its pure service. The best worship penetrates to that region where the things of sense cannot accompany men; where, with nothing to speak to the senses, the Eternal God in purest spirit is present in His supersensible glory.[108]

Worship was to be so focused upon the internal, that the external sense oriented aspects were undermined. Although he did not think of himself as creating a doctrine that would stifle, nonetheless his framework limited and suppressed creativity. This purity of worship and a connection with the God who exists beyond the senses was Calvin's goal, yet this fails to recognize that mankind was created as a total being and he runs, once again, into a Platonic Dualism that raises the value of the spirit and denigrates the value of the physical. Although Calvin did not mean to be "negative" in his attempt to solve the issue of freedom, the results of his restrictive doctrine led to stunted development in the creative arts within the Reformed movement. Both Luther and Calvin were concerned with freedom, however Luther thought in the direction of the freedom of expression toward God and Calvin thought more in line of restricting freedom in the world. One led to creativity, the other led to stunted creative endeavor.

This contrast between Luther and Calvin can also be seen in their trust of the senses. Luther balances freedom of the senses with a spiritual awareness of motives. As he writes to a young friend he commends music as a "noble, wholesome, and joyful creation, through which the feeling of your heart may at times be helped, especially when withstanding shameful lusts and bad company. Therefore accustom yourself to see in this creation your Creator and to praise Him through it. Diligently beware of corrupt hearts, which misuse this most beautiful and natural of gifts and art, as do those lascivious and lewd poets, who use it for their insane armours."[109] This balance gives freedom to hear music as it communicates the Word, as well as freedom to the individual to allow the Spirit of God to teach them through the music.

Peter Auksi draws in the idea of Calvin's "high view" of God as Creator and Lord in contrast to humanity's corruption. He writes, "Ultimately Calvinistic worship drives towards a religion where the flawed senses of corrupt man can neither apprehend nor cultivate the supersensible glory of God."[110] Calvin, however, focuses on the mistrust of the human senses to a point that he regulates them in a state of suppression. Rather than allowing the Spirit of God to train the senses in all that they perceive, he would rather restrict the sensory input since it might threaten "the still, inward and rational intensity of right worship, for they involved ceremonial symbols which could release the imagination into uncharitable digressions."[111] It was this total focus on limiting the senses that causes Calvin to have an imbalanced view. Certainly in today's culture the senses are often on overload, and the distraction that modern entertainment brings is unparalleled in history, so Calvin's point should not be overlooked in guarding the hearts and minds of believers. A balanced approach in this area, however, would be to teach discernment, as Luther desired, rather than restriction. A discerning heart is one that restricts itself, and with right motives.

There is no doubt that much can be learned from a continuing study of both Luther and Calvin in relation to music. Although Luther appears to have a much more balanced approach and philosophy concerning music, one cannot take lightly the constant emphasis and care that Calvin takes for protecting the heart of the worshiper. Either way, abuses can occur – on the one side toward the liberal use of texts and forms which once again obscure the message, and on the other side toward a confining legalism.

A Solid Foundation for a Theology of Music

The complexity of Martin Luther's theology is apparent even within the narrow confines and focus of this study. His theology of creation infiltrates his consideration of music and the arts as he recognizes the evidence of *order* that is inherent in music itself. His adherence and departure from the nominalism of his education will probably always frustrate scholars as they seek to understand Luther's significance in the midst of the Reformation.

We have seen how Luther's theology of music compares with the thought of two other great reformers, John Calvin and Huldrych Zwingli. Although there are some similarities in the underlying motives of their reforms, it was shown that Martin Luther established a more balanced approach in the area of music. It is with this in mind that the following observations are made.

Luther's theology in the area of music as it has been described in these chapters should serve as a basis for the modern church in a redevelopment of its own theology of music. Beyond that, it should also help in the formulation of a broader theology of the arts and a re-thinking of the church's theology concerning worship – both as a corporate act and an individual act.

The lack of a unified, carefully considered theology of music in today's evangelical circles has led to a plethora of abuses and misinterpretations of the role of music within the church. Rather than following a balanced approach grounded in Scripture, such as Luther's, there is evidence that the existential thought of Soren Kierkegaard is more influential in the modern church's worship, though this is barely noticed even in scholarly circles. The ideas of "praise prompting" and a "God in the gallery" mentality are shallow interpretations of Kierkegaard's thought that have much deeper and more significant implications. Though outside the bounds of this study, the point is made to encourage further study of Kierkegaard's influence on modern worship theology, and whether it adheres to a biblical norm. Is it appropriate at all to take a narrow, existential approach to worship, or would the modern church be better served by returning to a solid biblical theology of music and worship similar to Luther's?

Music, and the other arts, as creative acts are obvious examples of God's image in man. The distortion of these arts outside of the redeeming work of Christ in a person's life shows the need for the church to set free its artisans, musicians and actors to portray to the world God's Word, especially as it is revealed in the Living Word, Jesus Christ. The redemption of the aural, visual and other sensual faculties by the church can be a powerful example of redemption in Christ for the world to see, touch and hear. In this multidimensional, media-soaked culture the church must allow for innovative approaches for the presentation of the gospel. Within the parameters of returning to an understanding of order as perceived by Luther and shown in God's own creative activity, the arts can bring the Word to life in ways that the spoken or written word is unable.

Balance is also needed in the adaptation of cultural factors into church life, especially as it pertains to worship and music. Luther showed this possibility throughout his theology, and there seems to be no other solution to the tide of secularization that the church finds itself in today as it competes with the flash and polish of the modern media. This balance must be grounded in the biblical models and redeem any useful models from the culture insofar as they can be transformed by the Word. The church must carefully balance an adherence to historic Christianity, while still remaining relevant to the constantly changing culture it seeks to influence. It must balance a prayerful, obedient form of discipleship with the demands of modern ministry in a post-postmodern environment. It must listen first to the Spirit of God, and only then consider the possibilities from elsewhere and be careful, just as Luther and Calvin were, to protect the heart of the believer from things that may lead him or her away from the foundations of faith in Jesus Christ.

In the broadest sense, the church's worship will be transformed when it is allowed to flourish within God's own design. If multi-sensory worship is the wave of the future, as suggested by some today, then allowing freedom in the arts is the key to that future. The creative arts will transform musical praise, visual piety, the sermon, and even corporate prayer. In this creative freedom the liturgy of the church will transform as well, regardless of whether a particular congregation is committed to retain an historical liturgical form, or has a desire to allow worship to flow more freely. The forms of worship themselves will be a point of innovation. This would be in keeping with the spirit of Luther's open-armed and balanced approach to the arts based upon a solid theological foundation of God's creation, man's fall, and redemption offered in Jesus Christ.

Chapter 6

Luther's Doctrine of the Word

For Martin Luther, the Word of God was the foundation of theology. It was the assurance of God's Word upon which all of God's promises rested. Justification and the Christian life were the results of faith based upon God's Word. The Word of God became, for Luther, the dividing line between truth and error. He threw himself completely upon its veracity, and rested securely in all that it taught. In his own words, Luther put it this way, "Therefore we must take note of God's power that we may be completely without doubt about the things which God promises in His Word. Here full assurance is given concerning all His promises; nothing is either so difficult or so impossible that He could not bring it about by His Word."[112]

There were many ways in which Luther brought the Word of God to bear within his theological framework. He saw the Word as active in creation, theology and the Christian life. He, as one might expect, found the Word in flesh – incarnate in Jesus Christ. He relied upon and voiced his praise for the representation of God's Word in both of its oral forms in human language – that of Scripture, and of preaching. Luther saw the evidence of the Word of God in the sacraments and clarified its form there. This chapter will explore these aspects of Luther's doctrine of the Word of God as he considers them in various writings.

The Word of God as Active

Luther saw the Word of God as an active word. This is an inheritance from his Ockhamist/nominalistic background, especially as represented in Luther's "spiritual grandfather," Gabriel Biel. To the Ockhamist, God's Word established reality in all of its particulars. When God speaks, reality is established. This reality is not some representation of a heavenly reality, but it is a reality that is real – here and now. Although he testified that the "authority of Scripture meant nothing to Gabriel,"[113] Luther himself took Scripture seriously as the Word of God, as will be discussed later, and regarded faith and the Word to be the place in which true wisdom resides. "Therefore," he wrote, "in articles of faith one must have recourse to another dialectic and philosophy, which is called the word of God and faith."[114]

There appear to be at least three areas in which Luther recognized the Word of God being an active Word. The first is the Word as active in creation and preservation of His creation. Secondly, Luther found the active Word in the Law as condemning the sinner. Thirdly, the Word of God is active in the redemption and sanctification of the people of God. One may glimpse the pattern that modern theologians would refer to as "creation – fall – redemption" in Luther's doctrine of the Word as active in creation, condemnation and redemption.

The Word Active in Creation

As God spoke in creation, his Word actively created reality and one can find this represented in Luther's exposition of creation in the first chapters of Genesis. Over and over Moses wrote, "And God said...and it was so." For Luther, this is a significant example of God's Word establishing reality and creating, from nothing, all that exists. He clarified this by stating:

> Here attention must also be called to this, that the words "Let there be light" are the words of God, not of Moses; this means that they are realities. For God calls into existence the things which do not exist (Romans 4:17). He does not speak grammatical words; He speaks true and existent realities. Accordingly, that which among us has the sound of a word is a reality with God. Thus sun, moon, heaven, earth, Peter, Paul, I, you, etc. – we are all words of God, in fact only one single syllable or letter by comparison with the entire creation. We, too, speak, but only according to the rules of language, that is, we assign names to objects which have already been created. But the divine rule of language is different, namely: when He

says: "Sun, shine," the sun is there at once and shines. Thus the words of God are realities, not bare words.[115]

The creative activity of God through His Word did not stop, however, once the creative act was accomplished. To Luther, this active Word of God continued in His providential care and sustenance of His creatures. This is evident as he described God's preservation of the created world, through His Word, in preparation for the creation of man in his comments on Genesis 1:14, "...and our intellect must adjust itself to the Word of God and the Holy Scripture, which plainly teaches that God created all these things in order to prepare a house and an inn, as it were, for the future man, and that He governs and preserves these creatures by the power of His Word, by which He also created them."[116] Man is to learn from this creative and preserving activity of the Word, and recognize God's care as well. "Finally, then," Luther continued, "after everything that belongs to the essence of a house is ready, man is brought, as it were, into his possession that we may learn that the divine providence for us is greater than all our anxiety and care."[117] This element of providential care, and the comfort that it brings, is a common theme in Luther's theological insights. Here he found it in the creative activity of the Word.

The Word Active in Condemnation

Luther's distinction of Law and Gospel permeates his thought and theology. The distinction of proper righteousness ("proper" in the sense of coming from oneself) and alien righteousness ("alien" in being provided by another, i.e., by Christ) is closely related to Law and Gospel. The Law – God's law as a whole, whether moral, social or political – is a Law of proper righteousness. It is a Law that shows man that his own works fall short of making man righteous and acceptable before God. In this way it is the Word of God coming to the sinner with condemnation. Luther said, "The Law only shows sin, terrifies, and humbles; thus it prepares us for justification and drives us to Christ."[118] The Word of God in the Law is active in condemning and judging the sinner.

David Steinmetz makes an interesting point in his discussion on this aspect of Luther's theology of the Word. In balancing the ideas of both the hidden and revealed God, he also sees a balance in Law and Gospel in Luther's thinking. "The Word which the revealed God speaks is both Law and Gospel, both wrath and mercy, both no and yes. The Law no less than the Gospel is the Word of God. This law condemns me as a sinner in such a way that my conscience agrees with that judgment. Unless I can overcome God's 'no' spoken in the Law with God's 'yes' spoken in the Gospel, the last enemy to keep me from God will be God himself."[119] For Luther, this is the crushing reality of God's Word found in the Law. It condemns the sinner and leaves no hope – except the hope as found in Christ. In commenting on Galatians 3:20, Luther summarizes his view of the Law in this way:

> Therefore the Law cannot do anything except that with its light it illumines the conscience for sin, death, judgment, and the hate and wrath of God. Before the Law comes, I am smug and do not worry about sin; when the Law comes, it shows me sin, death and hell. Surely this is not being justified; it is being sentenced, being made an enemy of God, being condemned to death and hell. Therefore the principal purpose of the Law in theology is to make men not better but worse; that is, it shows them their sin, so that by the recognition of sin they may be humbled, frightened, and worn down, and so may long for grace and for the Blessed Offspring.[120]

So the Law, for Luther, condemns the sinner and drives him toward Christ and the Gospel.

The Word Active in Redemption

One can hardly read Luther's lectures, commentaries or sermons without also noticing the activity of God's Word in redemption. This is apparent in the way in which the active

Word is important in the assurance of God's promises. Since the Word of God establishes reality, then anything and everything He promised is established as well. For Luther, this is the basis of the assurance of salvation through faith in Christ. Although this concept (this "theology of the cross") is incomprehensible to reason, and foolishness to the wisdom of man, it is in fact the promise of God and the established reality of man's righteousness in Christ. Christ takes the sinner's sin and gives the sinner His own righteousness because God says it is so, and in that promise the believer can be assured of the truth of his own salvation.

God's promises are sure, "And this is our foundation," Luther declares, "the Gospel commands us to look, not at our own good deeds or perfection but at God Himself as He promises, and at Christ Himself, the Mediator."[121] The promises of God are found in His Word, and it is impossible outside of His Word to otherwise understand the motives and desires of God. Luther points out, "This Word makes us certain that God casts away all His wrath and hatred toward us when He gave His only Son for our sins."[122]

Luther noted the passive role the sinner is to take in salvation and contrasted it with the active role of the Word of God. He placed the burden of activity on God and said, "As a matter of fact, our knowing is more passive than active; that is, it is more a matter of being known than of knowing. Our 'activity' is to permit God to do His work in us; He gives the Word, and when we take hold of this by the faith that God gives, we are born as sons of God."[123] Redemption is the activity of God, not of man, and God performs this activity in, by, and through His Word.

The activity of God's Word in redemption is the activity of His Word for sanctification as well. Luther states, "This is why we continually teach that the knowledge of Christ and of faith is not a human work but utterly a divine gift; as God creates faith, so He preserves us in it. And just as He initially gives us faith through the Word, so later on He exercises, increases, strengthens, and perfects us by that Word."[124] Just as God sustains His creation by the Word, he sustains the new creation by His Word as well.

The Word of God in Flesh

For Luther, God was a God who revealed Himself in the unbecoming. This was known as the "theology of the cross."[125] The "theology of the cross" was Luther's view that God revealed Himself in foolishness, for the foolishness of God is beyond the wisdom of man. He saw this principle in the opening chapters of First Corinthians, and used it over and over to show that God's wisdom, in its foolishness, stood over and above man's reason.

To man it would seem foolish for God to send the Word, His Son, to become human flesh – but in God's wisdom that is exactly what He did. From crib, to cross, to crypt God subverted human understanding and His Word became flesh. Luther touched upon the Word as flesh in his commentary on Genesis chapter one, but thoroughly discussed it in his sermons on John chapter one. In commenting on Genesis 1:5 he said it this way: "Thus God reveals Himself to us as the Speaker who has with Him the uncreated Word, through whom He created the world and all things with the greatest ease, namely, by speaking."[126]

Luther really brought these thoughts into focus in his sermons on John. Right from the start of John 1:1 – "In the beginning was the Word, and the Word was with God, and God was the Word" – Luther drew together the words of Moses and the words of John in respect to the Word of God: "John's expression on this subject is far more succinct and vivid than that of Moses, whose book begins with these words: 'In the beginning God created the heavens and the earth...And God spoke a word, and there was light.' St. John got the idea from Moses; but he is far more explicit in his statement that in the very beginning – antedating the creation of the universe, of the heavens, of the earth, or of any other creature – the Word existed, that this Word was with God, that God was this Word, and that this Word had existed from all eternity."[127] Luther goes on to conclude that reason is unable to understand this doctrine, for it can only be accepted under the influence of the Holy Spirit.

In a beautifully crafted summary, Luther led his listeners through this difficult doctrine in such a way that it drew the attention and focus toward the Word of God in all of its fullness:

> Any attempt to fathom and comprehend such statements with human reason and understanding will avail nothing, for none of this has its source in the reason: that there was a Word in God before the world's creation, and that this Word was God; that, as John says further on, this same Word, the Only-begotten of the Father, full of grace and truth, rested in the Father's bosom or heart and became flesh; and that no one else had ever seen or known God, because the Word, who is God's only-begotten Son, rested in the bosom of the Father and revealed Him to us. Nothing but faith can comprehend this. Whoever refuses to accept it in faith, to believe it before he understands it, but insists on exploring it with his reason and his five senses, let him persist in this if he will. But our mind will never master this doctrine; it is far too lofty for our reason. Holy Writ assures us that faith alone can appropriate it. Let anyone who refuses to believe it let it alone. In the end only the Holy Spirit from heaven above can create listeners and pupils who accept this doctrine and believe that the Word is God, that God's Son is the Word, and that the Word became flesh, that He is also the Light who can illumine all men who come into the world, and that without this Light all is darkness.[128]

Luther packed a shadow of almost every major theological distinction that he brought to light in this one paragraph, yet it centers upon the Word. The Word was spoken by the Father, revealed in His Son, and brought to the believer in the Holy Spirit. (More insight into this Trinitarian aspect of Luther's doctrine of the Word will be considered in a later section.)

But why did the Word become flesh? In Luther's thought it can be said in this way – *pro me, pro nobis* – "for me, for us." The gift of God's Word, the gift of His promise, the gift of righteousness and salvation in Christ was for the benefit of the believer. "Thus the most precious treasure and the strongest consolation we Christians have is this: that the Word, the true and natural Son of God, became man, with flesh and blood like that of any other human; that He became incarnate for our sakes..."[129] This was a great comfort to Luther, and reinforced the special value that God placed on man, His greatest of creatures.

The Word of God in Oral Forms

Luther believed the Word was proclaimed in two significant ways, both of which he considered "oral" forms of the Word. The first was the proclamation of God's Word through the prophets and apostles, as recorded in Holy Scripture. The second was the proclamation of God's Word by preaching.

The Word as Scripture

Luther's commitment to the authority of Scripture was unwavering and decisive. He filtered his entire theology through the written Word, as well as his views on society, family, law, discipline, church policy, and whatever else he thoughtfully considered. For Luther, the Word of God as found in Scripture was the authority for the church, not the papacy or any church structure. "The Scripture is the record of the apostolic witness to Christ and is as such the decisive authority in the church."[130] Upon this foundation everything else was to be built.

His deep commitment to Scripture came to him both externally and internally. In taking the vow upon receiving his Doctorate in Bible, he bowed to Scriptural authority and committed to defending it against error. In his biography of Luther, Kittelson notes, "Luther took an oath on the Bible to teach only true doctrine and to report all who promoted falsehood."[131] This oath was a commitment he carried with him throughout his life.

Luther also found himself being redirected to Scripture as he defended his doctrinal and theological insights in the face of both Catholic and Protestant critics. "We ought to burn the more with zeal for the word of God," he urged his companions, "so that we ourselves may be certain about our doctrine and faith and that we may be prepared to respond."[132] These external pressures led Luther to defend, not himself so much as what he felt was the basis of evangelical thinking – the Gospel of Jesus Christ as found in Scripture. He said of his critics:

> Therefore when they minimize this issue in such a dishonest way, they give ample evidence of how highly they regard the majesty of the Word. If they believed that it is the Word of God, they would not play around with it this way. No, they would treat is with the utmost respect; they would put their faith in it without any disputing or doubting; and they would know that one Word of God is all and that all are one, that one doctrine is all doctrines and all are one, so that when one is lost all are eventually lost, because they belong together and are held together by a common bond.[133]

Gerhard Ebeling notes that Luther desired to bring his theology from the external study of the Word into the internal realm of life. In this process one can see the growing internal commitment Luther had for Scripture. "His preparatory work for his first commentary on the Psalms is a unique testimony to the way he strove to understand the scripture in such a way that it did not remain merely the letter, that is, something alien, remote and external, but became the Spirit, that is, something alive in the heart, which takes possession of man."[134]

As he strove to uphold his oath of the Doctorate, Luther also found internal motivation from Scripture itself as he studied. He found a text such as Galatians 1:9 drew his focus toward the Bible and oriented his theological framework toward the study of Scripture. Luther desired to hold firmly with Paul in his declaration of the gospel, and so, "With Paul, therefore, we boldly and confidently pronounce a curse upon any doctrine that does not agree with ours."[135] Luther clearly saw himself and his message in direct accord with Paul's message. In this way Luther made an internal, personal commitment to Scripture as the sole authority for that message. One can hear Luther himself telling his own hearers as he summarizes Paul's words in Galatians 1:9, "What you heard from me was the pure Word of God. Let only this stand. I myself do not want to be a different teacher of the Gospel from what I was, nor do I want you to be different pupils."[136] Ebeling notes, "For Luther, theology as the object of intellectual inquiry and theology as the sphere of a personal encounter, formed an indivisible unity."[137]

The Word in Preaching

The other oral form of the Word that Luther promoted was the proclamation of the Word of God in preaching. This was also an important aspect of Luther's doctrine of the Word. For Luther, the Word proclaimed was God speaking again to draw people to Himself (Romans 10:14). The faithful proclamation of the Word was of the highest calling. Althaus states, "All Luther's theological thinking presupposes the authority of Scripture. His theology is nothing more than an attempt to interpret the Scripture. Its form is basically exegesis."[138] "The spoken word always remains the basic from of the gospel. The Scripture has its source and exists for the sake of oral proclamation."[139]

For Luther, a lack of response to the preaching of the Word was no indication of its effectiveness. The preacher's calling was still to preach the Word as revealed in Scripture. "The fact that all do not believe the Word," he said, "or come to believe and to receive the Holy Spirit, through the Word, does not detract from the efficacy of the Gospel...It is my opinion that the preaching of God's Word is just as effective and powerful today and that it bears as much fruit in our time as in the days of Christ, John, and the apostles."[140] The reality in Luther's mind was that few were chosen to respond in faith.

In the life of the church the Word was preached, believed, professed and lived. The Word, in fact, is a vital evidence of the church itself. Luther said, "Wherever the substance of the Word and the sacraments abides, therefore, there the holy church is present."[141] In a narrow sense, at a minimum the Word of God must be present. Luther stated:

> And even if there were no other sign than this [word] alone, it would still suffice to prove that a Christian, holy people must exist there, for God's word cannot be without God's people, and conversely, God's people cannot be without God's word. Otherwise, who would preach or hear it preached, if there were no people of God? And what could or would God's people believe, if there were no word of God?
>
> ...It is enough for us to know how this chief holy possession purges, sustains, nourishes, strengthens, and protects the church, as St. Augustine also says, 'The church is begotten, cared for, nourished, and strengthened by the word of God.'[142]

Gerhard Ebeling points out, "The holy Scriptures and the present day intersect as it were at a single point, in the conscience that hears the word. It was Luther's concern that the word of God should be heard in this way."[143] Preaching, for Luther, was the primary way in which the Word of God could come to God's people, but also the method of choice chosen by God in Romans 10:14, for "Who can hear without a preacher?"

The Word of God in the Sacraments

Luther's view of, and commitment to, the Sacraments rested upon Scripture. He also saw the Word of God infused into the sacraments themselves. His insistence upon acknowledging only two Sacraments – Baptism and the Lord's Supper – was based upon finding only those two actually represented in the pages of the Bible and sanctioned by Christ. In this way one can see that the Word of God – Scripture – established the legitimacy of these sacraments. Luther said it this way, "The right use of the sacraments involves nothing more than believing that all will be as the sacraments promise and pledge through God's Word."[144] He intertwines the external elements of the sacraments with the internal working of faith in God's Word so that the sacraments, as part of daily life in medieval times, bring comfort to the believer. "It follows from this," Luther said, "that the sacraments, that is, the external words of God as spoken by a priest, are a truly great comfort and at the same time a visible sign of divine intent. We must cling to them with a staunch faith..."[145]

For Luther, however, it went beyond this. As the active Word of God, the statements made at Baptism and during the Lord's Supper brought the gospel to the participants. It was not the ritual that brought God's forgiveness, but the Word accompanying these cherished practices brought God's promise into life. The religious activity represented the Words, but only in the Word of God itself did God reveal Himself and give freely of the gift of righteousness and faith. Steinmetz notes, "By stressing the primacy of the Word, Luther wants to emphasize the responsive rather than the causative character of faith. God gives himself to us in baptism, in preaching, and in the eucharist whether or not we greet his gift with faith. Indeed, the very faith we have is itself the gift of God."[146]

The best place to see, in a succinct way, Luther's thoughts on how the Word of God is effectual within the external forms of the sacraments is in his explanations of them within *The Small Catechism*. First, in dealing with Baptism, Luther explains: "Baptism is not merely water, but it is water used according to God's command and connected with God's Word...It effects forgiveness of sins, delivers from death and the devil, and grants eternal salvation to all who believe, as the Word and promise of God declare."[147] This seems to be a great work that the water of Baptism can produce, but Luther immediately clarified by asking, "How can water produce such great effects?" His answer:

> It is not the water that produces these effects, but the Word of God connected with the water, and our faith which relies on

the Word of God connected with the water. For without the Word of God that water is merely water and no Baptism. But when connected with the Word of God it is a Baptism, that is, a gracious water of life and a washing of regeneration in the Holy Spirit, as St. Paul wrote to Titus (3:5-8), "He saved us by the washing of regeneration and renewal in the Holy Spirit, which he poured out upon us richly through Jesus Christ our Saviour, so that we might be justified by his grace and become heirs in hope of eternal life. The saying is sure."[148]

It is no wonder that, seeing how interconnected and intertwined the water of Baptism and the Word of God are in this explanation, that Luther would be so vehemently opposed to anyone who suggested any other interpretation – such as the Anabaptists claiming the illegitimacy of infant Baptism. For Luther, this was a direct assault upon the Word of God, not just water baptism.

As for the Lord's Supper, Luther once again clearly explained his viewpoint and the connection of the sacrament with the Word of God. Luther said the Sacrament of the Altar was, "Instituted by Christ Himself, it is the true body and blood of our Lord Jesus Christ, under the bread and wine, given to us Christians to eat and drink."[149] The benefits of the sacrament are found "in the words 'for you' and 'for the forgiveness of sins.' By these words the forgiveness of sins, life, and salvation are given to us in the sacrament, for where there is forgiveness of sins, there are also life and salvation."[150] Once again, Luther turns to the question, paralleling the question on Baptism, "How can bodily eating and drinking produce such great effects?" And his answer:

> The eating and drinking do not in themselves produce them, but the words "for you" and "for the forgiveness of sins." These words, when accompanied by the bodily eating and drinking, are the chief thing in the sacrament, and he who believes these words has what they say and declare: the forgiveness of sins.[151]

Another way, in which Luther clarified the distinction between the Word and water, or the Word and the elements, is in the terms "testament" and "sign." He wrote, "We may learn from this that in every promise of God two things are presented to us, the word and the sign, so that we are to understand the word to be the testament, but the sign to be the sacrament."[152] He noted, however, "As there is greater power in the word than in the sign, so there is greater power in the testament than in the sacrament; for a man can have and use the word or testament apart from the sign or sacrament."[153] This is truly a comfort for Luther, and one that he would desire for those under his care. At any time, as often as one desires, "I can set the words of Christ before me and with them feed and strengthen my faith as often as I choose. This is truly spiritual eating and drinking."[154]

Other Aspects of Luther's Doctrine of the Word
Trinitarian Aspects of the Doctrine

There seems to be a certain reflection of the Trinity in Luther's treatment of the Word of God. We have seen in passing that each member of the Trinity participates in the life-giving activity of the Word, but there may be more to it than that. Luther found God the Father speaking His Word, from which all creation came forth. The Father speaks the external Word that causes reality (the nominalistic leaning in Luther), both in creation and in salvation. His promise guarantees salvation for those who respond in faith.

The Word of God the Father is also that Word by which His Son became flesh. God willed for His Son (the Word) to take human form, and Christ was obedient to the Father's will. So Christ is the Word of God incarnate. He both reveals God's Word and is God's Word, but also is the fulfillment of God's Word. In this Luther reflects the creed which says Christ, the Word, is begotten of the Father.

The Holy Spirit, then, proceeds from the Father and Son. Through the Holy Spirit the Word becomes internal to the believer. The Holy Spirit takes the Word of God the Father, as it is revealed in Jesus Christ (i.e., the Gospel) and creates faith in the Word, which brings salvation to the sinner. Althaus notes, "God's word, however, is never merely an external word, spoken by human lips and heard with human ears. On the contrary, at the same time that this word is spoken, God speaks his truth in our hearts so that men receive it not only externally but also internally and believe it. This is the work of the Spirit of God."[155]

It may be that Luther is simply reflecting the influence that Augustine had on him. In commenting upon Genesis 1:20, Luther noted:

> Here we must deal also with what the holy fathers, and Augustine in particular, have noted, namely, that Moses employs these three words – "God said," "He made," "He saw" – as if in this manner he wanted to point to the three Persons of the Divine Majesty. By the term "He said" the Father is denoted. He begets the Word in eternity and in time establishes this world through that Word. Therefore they have attributed the verb "made" to the Person of the Son. The Son has in Himself not only the image of the Divine Majesty but also the image of all created things. Therefore He bestows existence on things. Just as the objects are spoken by the Father, so all things have their existence through the Son and the Word of the Father. To these, however, is joined the Third Person, the Holy Spirit, who "sees" the created things and approves them.
>
> The statements which beautifully and suitably assign these verbs were made for the purpose of understanding the doctrine of the Trinity more clearly. The sole reason why these helps were piously thought out by the holy fathers was this, to make somewhat comprehensible a matter which in itself is beyond comprehension. Therefore I do not find fault with those thoughts, since they are in accordance with the faith and are suitable and useful for strengthening and teaching our faith.[156]

In summary, God the Father speaks the Word. That Word is Christ, and the Holy Spirit brings this Word into the hearts of men. For Luther, this is a summary of the gospel and evidence of the active Word of God – active by the participation of each person of the Trinity.

The Christocentric Aspects of the Doctrine

Luther's conception of the Word of God is often difficult to squeeze into a particular mold. His exegesis of both the first chapter of Genesis and the first chapter of John revolves around the significance of Christ as the Word of God being a part of the creative activity of the Father, while at the same time becoming flesh and being truly man. The Word, or Christ, is eternally existent with the Father, and is one essence with the Father. The Word is God and the Word is Christ. God is the Word and God is Christ. This Word, Christ, also becomes flesh and dwells among men. Jesus is the Word of God who is both fully God and fully man. This leads to the conclusion that Luther's doctrine of the Word is thoroughly Christocentric.

Luther's references to the Word in these passages imply his insistence that the Gospel is central to God's Word of promise. In other words, the message of Christ (the Word) is God's promise (His Word) to exchange the sinner's sin for the righteousness of Christ – this is the Gospel. This is the message of Scripture (the Word of God), and the proclamation of the church (through preaching and the sacraments – transmission of the Word to God's people). If Luther's theology is Christocentric, as most historians and students of his writings conclude, then his doctrine of the Word is as thoroughly Christocentric as possible.

Luther confirmed this in his Romans lectures by stating, "Here the door is thrown open wide for the understanding of Holy Scripture, that is, that everything must be understood in relation to Christ..."[157] He also confirmed it in the 1535 preface to the publication of his Galatians lectures by writing, "For in my heart there rules this one doctrine, namely, faith in Christ. From it, through it, and to it all my theological thought flows and returns, day and night..."[158]

Paul Althaus writes, "Christ is the incarnate Word of God. Therefore the Bible can be the word of God only if its sole and entire content is Christ."[159] Althaus continues in clarification:

> This does not mean that the Holy Scripture contains exclusively gospel. According to Luther, its content is both law and gospel. And Christ is the interpreter of the law. As far as the Scripture presents law, it drives men forward to Christ as the Savior. For the law is given as a preparation for Christ and drives men toward him. Thus the Scripture as law and gospel, indirectly and directly, bears witness to Christ. And it is in this sense that Christ is its sole and total content. Understood in this way, Scripture is a unity. Not everything in the Holy Scriptures is gospel, but it contains the gospel in all its parts; and where it is law it still directs men toward the gospel.[160]

In Althaus' analysis, this Christocentric view is emphatically evident. He notes, again, "One can formulate Luther's principle thus: Scripture is always to be interpreted according to the analogy of Scripture. And this is nothing else than the analogy of the gospel. Christocentric interpretation for Luther thus means gospel-centered interpretation, understood in terms of the gospel of justification by faith alone."[161] This is obvious from Luther himself as he stated, "*The Gospel* is not only what Matthew, Mark, Luke, and John have written. This is clear enough from this passage (Romans 1:3-4). For it states expressly that the Gospel is the Word concerning the Son of God, who became flesh, suffered, and was glorified."[162]

It is apparent that, in Luther's mind, the doctrine of the Word cannot be separated from the doctrine of the Person of Christ. The two are inseparable as representations of the active Word of God.

Conclusion

It has been clearly shown that Martin Luther's doctrine of the Word of God is complex but thorough. This chapter considered the many ways in which Luther brought the Word of God to bear within his theological framework. He saw the Word as active. He saw the Word as flesh. He saw the Word in oral forms, and He saw the Word in the sacraments. It was noted that his view of the Word of God was both Trinitarian and thoroughly Christocentric.

Luther's doctrine of the Word is a foundational aspect of his theology and forms a foundation upon which the rest of his theology is built. One could only hope that that modern theologians and the modern church would take the Word of God as seriously, and with such deep conviction.

Notes

Chapter 1 – The Theology of the Reformers and Their Hymns

[1] Teresa Berger, *Theology in Hymns?* (Nashville: Kingswood Books, 1989), 20-21.

[2] James F. White in *The Complete Library of Christian Worship, Vol. 2: Twenty Centuries of Christian Worship*, Robert Webber, ed. (Nashville: Star Song Publishing Group, 1994), 75.

[3] Martin Luther, *Luther's Works, Volume 49: Letters II*, ed. and trans. Gottfried G. Krodel (Philadelphia: Fortress Press, 1972), 68.

[4] Paul Nettl, *Luther and Music* (New York: Russell and Russell, 1967), 39.

[5] Evelyn C. Schuette, "The Reformation and Musical Influences on Martin Luther's Early Protestant Hymnody," *Reformed Liturgy and Music*, 16 (Summer 1982), 99-106.

[6] Schuette, "Reformation and Musical Influences," 102.

[7] Nettl, *Luther and Music*, 2.

[8] John D. Witvliet, "The Spirituality of the Psalter: Metrical Psalms in Liturgy and Life in Calvin's Geneva," *Calvin Theological Journal*, 32 (November 1997), 280-282.

[9] Nathaniel Micklem, ed. *Christian Worship: Studies in its History and Meaning* (London: Oxford University Press, 1936), 162.

[10] Witvliet, "The Spirituality of the Psalter," 282.

[11] E. E. Ryden, *The Story of Christian Hymnody* (Rock Island, IL: Augustana Press, 1959), 109.

[12] Witvliet, "The Spirituality of the Psalter," 282.

[13] Charles Garside, *Zwingli and the Arts* (New Haven and London: Yale University Press, 1966), 45.

[14] Donald P. Hustad, *Jubilate! Church Music in the Evangelical Tradition* (Carol Stream, IL: Hope Publishing Company, 1952), 114.

[15] Garside, *Zwingli and the Arts*, 41.

[16] Quoted by Garside, *Zwingli and the Arts*, 42.

[17] Garside, *Zwingli and the Arts*, 42-43.

[18] Berenard Kreuzer, " A Study of 16th and 17th Century Protestant German Hymnody," (University of Iowa Dissertation, December 1973), 126-127.

19 Oliver C. Rupprecht, "Theological and Musical Riches of a
Reformation Hymn," *Concordia Journal*, 11 (Summer 1985), 167.

Chapter 2 – Luther's Theology of Music

20 The number of authors who recognize this in Luther's writings
would be too numerous to quote here, but as a representative list,
the following would suffice: Paul Althaus, *The Theology of Martin
Luther* (Philadelphia: Fortress Press, 1966): 115-118; Peter Auksi,
"Simplicity and silence: The influence of Scripture on the
aesthetic thought of the major reformers," *Journal of Religious
History*, Volume 10 (1979): 343-364; Heinrich Bornkamm, *The
Heart of Reformation Faith* (New York: Harper and Row, 1965);
Charles Garside, "Some Attitudes of the major Reformers toward
the role of music in the liturgy," *McCormick Quarterly*
(November 1967): 151-168; Robin A. Leaver, "Theological
Consistency, Liturgical Integrity, and Musical Hermeneutics in
Luther's Liturgical Reforms," *Lutheran Quarterly* (Summer
1995): 117-138; James Mackinnon, *Luther and the Reformation*
(New York: Russell & Russell, Inc., 1962); Paul Nettl, *Luther and
Music* (Philadelphia: The Muhlenburg Press, 1948); and Carl F.
Schalk, *Luther on Music, Paradigms of Praise* (St. Louis:
Concordia Publishing House, 1988).

21 Brian L Horne, "A Civitas of Sound: On Luther and Music,"
Theology (January 1985), 21-28.

22 Horne, A Civitas of Sound, 27.

23 Paul Althaus, *The Theology of Martin Luther* (Philadelphia:
Fortress Press, 1966), 117-118.

24 Charles Garside, "Some Attitudes of the major Reformers toward
the role of music in the liturgy," *McCormick Quarterly*
(November 1967), 163.

25 The differences between Calvin's Reformed musical heritage and
Luther's heritage in the development in Western music are very
apparent, and will be discussed in Chapter 4. Some representative
studies would include: Peter Auksi, "Regenerate Art: The Major
Reformers" in *The Christian Plain Style: The Evolution of a
Spiritual Ideal* (Montreal and Kingston: McGill-Queen's
University Press, 1995): 203-330; Adrienne Thompson Bailey,
"Music in the Liturgies of the Reformers: Martin Luther and Jean
Calvin," *Reformed Liturgy and Music*, Vol. 21 (1987): 74-79;

Charles Garside, Jr., *The Origins of Calvin's Theology of Music: 1536-1543* (Philadelphia: The American Philosophical Society, August 1979); and Nathaniel Micklem, ed., *Christian Worship, Studies in its History and Meaning* (London: Oxford University Press, 1938).
Zwingli's views were so restrictive of music and creativity for use by the church that he is usually not part of the comparative studies as are Luther and Calvin. For the best representation of his views see Charles Garside, *Zwingli and the Arts* (New Haven and London: Yale University Press, 1966).

[26] Luther discusses music primarily and considers it the pre-eminent creative activity, but does not exclude the other arts as evidence of God's creativity and order, though his discussion of them is limited.

Chapter 3 – Creation and Music in Luther's Theology

[27] In addition to the footnoted items, the discussion of medieval scholasticism is a synopsis from: Michael Wittmer, *Seminar Lectures and Notes on Medieval Theology* (Grand Rapids Theological Seminary, Spring 2002).

[28] Etienne Gilson, *Reason and Revelation in the Middle Ages* (New York: Charles Scribner's Sons, 1938), 20.

[29] Gilson, Reason and Revelation, 59.

[30] David Knowles, *The Evolution of Medieval Thought* (Baltimore: Helicon Press, 1962), 332.

[31] Augustine, "The Nature of the Good, Against the Manichees," in *The Library of Christian Classics, Vol. VI: Augustine: Earlier Writings*, ed. by John H.S. Burleigh. (Philadelphia: The Westminster Press, 1953), 327.

[32] Knowles, *Evolution*, 332.

[33] Martin Luther, *Luther's Works, Volume 1: Lectures on Genesis 1-5*, Edited by Jaroslav Pelikan, trans. by George V. Schick (St. Louis: Concordia Publishing House, 1958), 5.

[34] Heiko Oberman, *The Harvest of Medieval Theology: Gabriel Biel and Late Medieval Nominalism* (Durham, NC: The Labyrinth Press, 1983), 74.

[35] Paul Althaus, *The Theology of Martin Luther*, 4.

[36] Luther, *Genesis*, 35.

[37] Luther, *Genesis*, 32-33.

38 Luther, *Genesis*, 42.
39 Luther, *Genesis*, 125.
40 Luther, *Genesis*, 57.
41 Luther, *Genesis*, 61.
42 Luther, *Genesis*, 67.
43 Luther, *Genesis*, 131.
44 Luther, *Genesis*, 141.
45 Luther, *Genesis*, 141.
46 Luther, *Genesis*, 143.
47 Luther, *Genesis*, 55.
48 Theodore Hoelty-Nickel, "Luther and Music," in *Luther and Culture: Martin Luther Lectures, Volume 4.* (Decorah, Iowa: Luther College Press, 1960), 149.
49 Hoelty-Nickel, "Luther and Music," 151.
50 Hoelty-Nickel, "Luther and Music," 156.
51 Charles Garside, "Some Attitudes of the major Reformers toward the role of music in the liturgy," *McCormick Quarterly* (November 1967), 153.
52 For a sketch of Luther's support of Melancthon's theological writings see Clyde L. Manschrek, "An Historical Note" in the Preface of *Melanchthon on Christian Doctrine: Loci Communes 1555,* edited and trans. by Clyde L. Manschreck (New York: Oxford University Press, 1965), vii-xxiv.
53 Paul Henry Lang, *Music in Western Civilization* (New York: W. W. Norton & Co., Inc., 1941), 208.

Chapter 4 – Luther's Theology in Context

54 Martin Luther, *Luther's Works, Volume 49: Letters II,* ed. and trans. Gottfried G. Krodel (Philadelphia: Fortress Press, 1972), 68.
55 Peter Auksi, "Simplicity and silence: The influence of Scripture on the aesthetic thought of the major reformers," *Journal of Religious History,* Volume 10 (1979), 350.
56 John Calvin, *Institutes of the Christian Religion,* 2 Vol., ed. J.T. McNeil, trans F.L. Battles (Philadelphia: The Westminster Press, 1960), 896.
57 Martin Luther, *Luther's Works, Volume 53: Liturgy and Hymns,* ed. Ulrich S. Leupold (Philadelphia: Fortress Press, 1965), 323-324.

[58] John Calvin, "Letter to the Reader" in *The Form of Prayers and Songs of the Church 1542*, trans. Ford Lewis Battles, *Calvin Theological Journal* (Volume 15, Number 2, 1980), 163.

[59] Charles Garside, Jr., *The Origins of Calvin's Theology of Music: 1536-1543* (The American Philosophical Society, Philadelphia: August 1979), 13.

[60] Luther, *Luther's Works, Volume 53: Liturgy and Hymns*, 332.

[61] Luther, *Luther's Works, Volume 53: Liturgy and Hymns*, 327-328.

[62] Peter Auksi, "Regenerate Art: The Major Reformers," *The Christian Plain Style: The Evolution of a Spiritual Ideal* (Montreal and Kingston: McGill-Queen's University Press, 1995), 217.

[63] Luther, *Luther's Works, Volume 53: Liturgy and Hymns*, 316.

[64] Calvin, *Institutes of the Christian Religion*, 895-896.

[65] Charles Garside, *Zwingli and the Arts* (New Haven and London: Yale University Press, 1966), 45.

[66] Donald P Hustad, *Jubilate! Church Music in the Evangelical Tradition* (Carol Stream, IL: Hope Publishing Company, 1952), 114.

[67] Garside, *Zwingli*, 41.

[68] Huldrych Zwingli, *Writings, Volume I: The Defense of the Reformed Faith*, trans. E.J. Furcha, (Allison Park, PA: Pickwick Publications, 1984), 181.

[69] Garside, *Zwingli*, 42-43.

[70] W.P. Stephens, *The Theology of Huldrych Zwingli* (Oxford: Clarendon Press, 1986), 6.

[71] Stephens, *Zwingli*, 45.

[72] Ulrich Zwingli, *On Providence and Other Essays*, ed. by William John Hinke (Durham, North Carolina: The Labyrinth Press, 1983), 160.

[73] Zwingli, *On Providence*, 161-162.

[74] Auksi, "Simplicity and silence," 349.

[75] Luther, Luther's Works, Volume 53: Liturgy and Hymns, 315-316.

[76] John Calvin, *Calvin's Commentaries: The Gospel according to St. John 1-10*, eds. David W. Torrance and Thomas F. Torrance, trans. T.H.L. Parker (Grand Rapids: Wm. B. Eerdmans Publishing Company, 1959), 101.

[77] Calvin, *Gospel according to St. John*, 101.

[78] Charles Garside, "Some Attitudes," 163.

[79] Calvin, "Letter to the Reader," 161-163.

80 Calvin, *Institutes of the Christian Religion*, 184.
81 Calvin, *Institutes of the Christian Religion*, 184-185.
82 Calvin, *Institutes of the Christian Religion*, 186.
83 Augustine, *The Confessions*, trans. Henry Chadwick, (Oxford: Oxford University Press, 1998), 208.
84 Quote of Martin Luther, trans. by Walter E. Buszin, in *Luther on Music* (Saint Paul: North Central Publishing Company, 1958), 11. Buszin notes the translation as originating from the Erlangen edition of Luther's Works, LXII, 111.
85 Buszin, *Luther on Music*, 11.
86 James Rawlings Sydnor, "Hymnody: Sung Prayer," *Reformed Liturgy and Music* (Fall 1992), 185.
87 Garside, "Some Attitudes," 161.
88 Garside, "Some Attitudes," 163.
89 Luther, *Luther's Works, Volume 53: Liturgy and Hymns*, 327.
90 Calvin, "Letter to the Reader," 164.
91 Garside, "Some Attitudes," 161.
92 Garside, "Some Attitudes," 162.
93 Garside, "Some Attitudes," 164.
94 Luther, *Luther's Works, Volume 53: Liturgy and Hymns*, 322.
95 Garside, *The Origins of Calvin's Theology of Music*, 19.
96 Garside, "Some Attitudes," 162.
97 Calvin, *Gospel according to St. John*, 100-101.
98 Garside, *The Origins of Calvin's Theology of Music*, 19.

Chapter 5 – A Comprehensive and Balanced View

99 Luther, *Luther's Works, Volume 53: Liturgy and Hymns*, 316.
100 Luther, *Luther's Works, Volume 49: Letters II*, 428.
101 Auksi, "Regenerate Art: The Major Reformers," 205.
102 Nathaniel Micklem, ed., *Christian Worship, Studies in its History and Meaning* (London: Oxford University Press, 1938), 161.
103 Auksi, "Regenerate Art: The Major Reformers," 204.
104 Calvin, *Gospel according to St. John*, 101.
105 Auksi, "Regenerate Art: The Major Reformers," 216.
106 Auksi, "Regenerate Art: The Major Reformers," 207.
107 Paul Nettl, *Luther and Music* (Philadelphia: The Muhlenburg Press, 1948), 18.
108 Micklem, ed., *Christian Worship*, 162.
109 Luther, *Luther's Works, Volume 53: Liturgy and Hymns*, 324.

[110] Auksi, "Simplicity and silence," 353.

[111] Auksi, "Simplicity and silence," 353.

Chapter 6 – Martin Luther's Doctrine of the Word of God

[112] Martin Luther, *Luther's Works, Vol. 1: Lectures on Genesis 1-5*, ed. by Jaroslav Pelikan, trans. by George V. Schick (St. Louis: Concordia Publishing House, 1958), 49.

[113] Martin Luther, *Luther's Works, Vol. 54: Table Talk*, ed. and trans. by Theodore G. Tappert (Philadelphia: Fortress Press, 1967), 264.

[114] Martin Luther, "The Disputation Concerning the Passage: 'The Word was Made Flesh' (John 1:14)" in *Luther's Works, Vol. 38: Word and Sacrament IV*, ed. and trans. by Martin E. Lehman (Philadelphia: Fortress Press, 1971), 241.

[115] Luther, *Genesis*, 21-22.

[116] Luther, *Genesis*, 47.

[117] Luther, *Genesis*, 47.

[118] Martin Luther, *Luther's Works, Vol. 26: Lectures on Galatians 1-4, 1535*, ed. by Jaroslav Pelikan and Walter Hansen, trans. by Jaroslav Pelikan (St. Louis: Concordia Publishing House, 1963), 126.

[119] David C. Steinmetz, *Luther in Context* (Bloomington: Indiana University Press, 1986), 29.

[120] Luther, *Galatians 1-4*, 327.

[121] Luther, *Galatians 1-4*, 387.

[122] Luther, *Galatians 1-4*, 388.

[123] Luther, *Galatians 1-4*, 401.

[124] Luther, *Galatians 1-4*, 64.

[125] Martin Luther, *Martin Luther's Basic Theological Writings*, ed. by Timothy F. Lull (Minneapolis: Fortress Press, 1989), 31-32.

[126] Luther, *Genesis*, 22.

[127] Martin Luther, *Luther's Works, Vol. 22: Sermons on the Gospel of St. John 1-4*, ed. by Jaroslav Pelikan, trans. by Martin H. Bertram (St. Louis: Concordia Publishing House, 1957), 7-8.

[128] Luther, *John*, 8.

[129] Luther, *John*, 110.

[130] Paul Althaus, *The Theology of Martin Luther*, trans. by Robert C. Schultz (Philadelphia: Fortress Press, 1966), 5.

[131] James M. Kittelson, *Luther: The Reformer* (Minneapolis: Augsburg Publishing House, 1986), 85.

[132] Luther, Disputation on Word made Flesh, 243.
[133] Martin Luther, *Luther's Works, Vol. 27: Lectures on Galatians 5-6, 1535 and Lectures on Galatians 1-6, 1519*, ed. by Pelikan and Hansen, trans. by Jaroslav Pelikan (St. Louis: Concordia Publishing House, 1964), 38.
[134] Gerhard Ebeling, *Luther: An Introduction to His Thought*, trans. by R.A. Wilson (Philadelphia: Fortress Press, 1970), 98.
[135] Luther, *Galatians 1-4*, 59.
[136] Luther, *Galatians 1-4*, 56.
[137] Ebeling, *Luther*, 95-96.
[138] Althaus, *Theology of Luther*, 3.
[139] Althaus, *Theology of Luther*, 72.
[140] Luther, *John*, 55.
[141] Luther, *Galatians 1-4*, 25.
[142] Luther, *Basic Writings*, 547-548.
[143] Ebeling, *Luther*, 58.
[144] Luther, *Basic Writings*, 650.
[145] Luther, *Basic Writings*, 647-648.
[146] Steinmetz, *Luther in Context*, 83.
[147] Luther, *Basic Writings*, 484-485.
[148] Luther, *Basic Writings*, 485.
[149] Luther, *Basic Writings*, 488.
[150] Luther, *Basic Writings*, 489.
[151] Luther, *Basic Writings*, 489.
[152] Luther, *Basic Writings*, 300.
[153] Luther, *Basic Writings*, 300.
[154] Luther, *Basic Writings*, 300.
[155] Althaus, *Theology of Luther*, 36.
[156] Luther, *Genesis*, 49-50.
[157] Martin Luther, *Luther's Works, Vol. 25: Lectures on Romans*, ed. by Hilton C. Oswald, trans. by Walter G. Tillmanns and Jacob A. O. Preus (St. Louis: Concordia Publishing House, 1972), 4.
[158] Luther, *Galatians 5-6*, 145.
[159] Althaus, *Theology of Luther*, 74.
[160] Althaus, *Theology of Luther*, 74.
[161] Althaus, *Theology of Luther*, 79.
[162] Luther, *Romans*, 148.

***

Bibliography

Primary Sources

Augustine. *The Confessions*. Translated by Henry Chadwick. Oxford: Oxford University Press, 1998.

Augustine. "The Nature of the Good, Against the Manichees." Pages 326-348 in *The Library of Christian Classics, Vol. VI: Augustine: Earlier Writings*. Edited by John H.S. Burleigh. Philadelphia: The Westminster Press, 1953.

Calvin, John. *Calvin's Commentaries: The Gospel according to St. John 1-10*. Edited by David W. Torrance and Thomas F. Torrance, translated by T.H.L. Parker. Grand Rapids: Wm. B. Eerdmans Publishing Company, 1959.

_____. "On the Creation of Man." Pages 186-204 in *Valiant for the Truth: A Treasury of Evangelical Writings*. Compiled and edited by David Otis Fuller. New York: McGraw-Hill Book Company, Inc., 1961.

_____. *Institutes of the Christian Religion*, Volumes 1 and 2. Edited by J.T. McNeil, translated by F.L. Battles. Philadelphia: The Westminster Press, 1960.

_____. "Letter to the Reader" in *The Form of Prayers and Songs of the Church 1542*. Translated by Ford Lewis Battles. *Calvin Theological Journal* (Volume 15, Number 2, 1980): 160-165.

Luther, Martin. *Luther's Works, Volume 1: Lectures on Genesis 1-5*. Edited by Jaroslav Pelikan, translated by George V. Schick. St. Louis: Concordia Publishing House, 1958.

_____. *Luther's Works, Vol. 22: Sermons on the Gospel of St. John 1-4*. Edited by Jaroslav Pelikan, translated by Martin H. Bertram. St. Louis: Concordia Publishing House, 1957.

_____. *Luther's Works, Vol. 25: Lectures on Romans*. Edited by Hilton C. Oswald, translated by Walter G. Tillmanns and Jacob A. O. Preus. St. Louis: Concordia Publishing House, 1972.

_____. *Luther's Works, Vol. 26: Lectures on Galatians 1-4, 1535*. Edited by Jaroslav Pelikan and Walter Hansen, translated by Jaroslav Pelikan. St. Louis: Concordia Publishing House, 1963.

_____. *Luther's Works, Vol. 27: Lectures on Galatians 5-6, 1535 and Lectures on Galatians 1- 6, 1519*. Edited by Jaroslav Pelikan and Walter Hansen, translated by Jaroslav Pelikan. St. Louis: Concordia Publishing House, 1964.

_____. *Luther's Works, Vol. 38: Word and Sacrament IV*. "The Disputation Concerning the Passage: 'The Word was Made Flesh' (John 1:14)." Edited and translated by Martin E. Lehman. Philadelphia: Fortress Press, 1971.

_____. *Luther's Works, Volume 49: Letters II*. Edited and translated by Gottfried G. Krodel. Philadelphia: Fortress Press, 1972.

_____. *Luther's Works, Volume 53: Liturgy and Hymns*. Edited by Ulrich S. Leupold. Philadelphia: Fortress Press, 1965.

_____. *Luther's Works, Vol. 54: Table Talk.* Edited and translated by Theodore G. Tappert. Philadelphia: Fortress Press, 1967.

_____. *Martin Luther's Basic Theological Writings.* Edited by Timothy F. Lull. Minneapolis: Fortress Press, 1989.

Zwingli, Ulrich. *On Providence and Other Essays.* Edited by William John Hinke. Durham, North Carolina: The Labyrinth Press, 1983.

_____. *Writings, Volume I: The Defense of the Reformed Faith.* Translated by E.J. Furcha. Allison Park, PA: Pickwick Publications, 1984.

Secondary Sources

Althaus, Paul. *The Theology of Martin Luther.* Trans. by Robert C. Schultz. Philadelphia: Fortress Press, 1966.

Anderson, Daniel L. "The Theology of German Anabaptism as Seen Through the Hymnody of its Major Forefathers." Dallas Theological Seminary, Dissertations and Theses, 1976.

Auksi, Peter. "Regenerate Art: The Major Reformers." Pages 203-330 in *The Christian Plain Style: The Evolution of a Spiritual Ideal.* Montreal and Kingston: McGill-Queen's University Press, 1995.

_____. "Simplicity and silence: The influence of Scripture on the aesthetic thought of the major reformers." *Journal of Religious History*, Volume 10 (1979): 343-364.

Bailey, Adrienne Thompson. "Music in the Liturgies of the Reformers: Martin Luther and Jean Calvin." *Reformed Liturgy and Music*, Vol. 21 (1987): 74-79.

Berger, Teresa. *Theology in Hymns?* Nashville: Kingswood Books, 1989.

Bornkamm, Heinrich. *The Heart of Reformation Faith*. New York: Harper and Row, 1965.

Brecht, Martin. "The Songs of the Anabaptists in Munster and Their hymnbook," *Mennonite Quarterly review*, 59 (October 1985): 362-366.

Breed, David R. *The History and Use of Hymns and Hymn-Tunes*. New York: Fleming H. Revell Company, 1903.

Buszin, Walter E. *Luther on Music*. Saint Paul: North Central Publishing Company, 1958.

Ebeling, Gerhard. *Luther: An Introduction to His Thought*. Trans. by R.A. Wilson. Philadelphia: Fortress Press, 1970.

Garside, Charles Jr. *The Origins of Calvin's Theology of Music: 1536-1543*. Philadelphia: The American Philosophical Society, August 1979.

_____. *Zwingli and the Arts*. New Haven and London: Yale University Press, 1966.

_____. "Some Attitudes of the major Reformers toward the role of music in the liturgy." *McCormick Quarterly* (November 1967): 151-168.

Gilson, Etienne. *Reason and Revelation in the Middle Ages.* New York: Charles Scribner's Sons, 1938.

Hoelty-Nickel, Theodore. "Luther and Music." In *Luther and Culture: Martin Luther Lectures, Volume 4.* Decorah, Iowa: Luther College Press, 1960.

Horne, Brian L. "A Civitas of Sound: On Luther and Music." *Theology* (January 1985): 21-28.

Hustad, Donald P. *Jubilate! Church Music in the Evangelical Tradition.* Carol Stream, IL: Hope Publishing Company, 1952.

Kittelson, James M. *Luther: The Reformer.* Minneapolis: Augsburg Publishing House, 1986.

Knowles, David. *The Evolution of Medieval Thought.* Baltimore: Helicon Press, 1962.

Kreuzer, Bernard. "A Study of 16th and 17th Century Protestant German Hymnody." University of Iowa Dissertation, December 1973.

Lambert, James F. *Luther's Hymns.* Philadelphia: General Council Publication House, 1917.

Lang, Paul Henry. *Music in Western Civilization.* New York: W. W. Norton & Co., Inc., 1941.

Leaver, Robin A. "Theological Consistency, Liturgical Integrity, and Musical Hermeneutics in Luther's Liturgical Reforms." *Lutheran Quarterly* (Summer 1995): 117-138.

Liechty, Daniel, ed. and trans. *Early Anabaptist Spirituality: Selected Writings.* New York: Paulist Press, 1994.

Mackinnon, James. *Luther and the Reformation.* New York: Russell & Russell, Inc., 1962.

Manwaring, Randle. "A Study of Hymn-Writing and Hymn-Singing in the Christian Church," *Texts and Studies in Religion Series.* Lewiston: The Edwin Mellen Press, 1990.

Melanchthon, Philip. *Melanchthon on Christian Doctrine: Loci Communes 1555.* Edited and translated by Clyde L. Manschreck. New York: Oxford University Press, 1965.

Micklem, Nathaniel, ed. *Christian Worship, Studies in its History and Meaning.* London: Oxford University Press, 1938.

Mullinax, Allen. "Martin Bucer and the Strasbourg Songbook: 1541." Southern Baptist Theological Seminary Thesis, December 1984.

Nettl, Paul. *Luther and Music.* Philadelphia: The Muhlenburg Press, 1948.

_____. *Luther and Music.* New York: Russell and Russell, 1967.

Niesel, Wilhelm. *The Theology of Calvin.* Philadelphia: The Westminster Press, 1956.

Oberman, Heiko A. *The Harvest of Medieval Theology: Gabriel Biel and Late Medieval Nominalism.* Durham, NC: The Labyrinth Press, 1983.

Routley, Erik. *A Panorama of Christian Hymnody.* Collegeville, MN: The Liturgical Press, 1979.

Rupprecht, Oliver C. "Theological and Musical Riches in a Reformation Hymn," *Concordia Journal,* 11 (Summer 1985): 164-179.

Ryden, E. E. *The Story of Christian Hymnody.* Rock Island, IL: Augustana Press, 1959.

Schalk, Carl F. *Luther on Music, Paradigms of Praise.* St. Louis: Concordia Publishing House, 1988.

Schuette, Evelyn C. "The Reformation and Musical Influences on Martin Luther's Early Protestant Hymnody," *Reformed Liturgy and Music,* 16 (Summer 1982): 99-106.

Steinmetz, David C. *Luther in Context.* Bloomington: Indiana University Press, 1986.

Stephens, W. P. *The Theology of Huldrych Zwingli.* Oxford: Clarendon Press, 1986.

Sydnor, James Rawlings. "Hymnody: Sung Prayer," *Reformed Liturgy and Music* (Fall 1992): 184-188.

Webber, Robert E. *Worship Old and New.* Grand Rapids: Zondervan Publishing House, 1982.

White, James F. in *The Complete Library of Christian Worship, Vol. 2: Twenty Centuries of Christian Worship.* Edited by Robert Webber. Nashville: Star Song Publishing Group, 1994.

Wittmer, Michael. *Lectures and Notes on Medieval Theology.* Grand Rapids Baptist Seminary: Spring 2002.

Witvliet, John D. "The Spirituality of the Psalter: Metrical Psalms in Liturgy and Life in Calvin's Geneva," *Calvin Theological Journal,* 32 (November 1997): 273-297.

Zinckgraf, June B. "The Music of the French Reformation in the 16th Century." Union Theological Seminary Thesis, April 1948.

About the Author

Mark Sooy is a pastor, teacher, theologian, worship leader, and musician. His experience has led him through opportunities in pastoral church ministry, Bible college instruction, worship leading, authoring, conference speaking and leading, emergent church ministry, and other forms of Christian service.

Mark holds a Bachelor of Theology degree with an emphasis in Pastoral Studies from Grace Bible College, as well as a Master of Arts in Historical Theology from Grand Rapids Theological Seminary of Cornerstone University. Both institutions are located in Grand Rapids, Michigan.

His other work includes articles for periodical publications, as well as the book *The Life of Worship: Rethink, Reform, Renew* – which is a discussion of the biblical, theological and lifestyle aspects of worship.

His wife, Elisabeth, often works alongside Mark in the various ministry opportunities that come their way. They currently reside in West Michigan with their three children: Estelle, Ashlea and Gordon.

For further information about Mark or Elisabeth and their ministries please visit: www.MarkSooy.com. You will find links to other resources, a place to sign up for their e-Newsletter, and other information that may be of interest.

You are also welcome to email Mark at mark@MarkSooy.com.

CPSIA information can be obtained
at www.ICGtesting.com
Printed in the USA
FFOW03n0958200118
44500664-44317FF